GATHERINGS
from
Grave Yards

PARTICULARLY THOSE OF LONDON.

With a concise History of the modes of Interment, among different Nations from the earliest periods

AND A DETAIL OF DANGEROUS & FATAL RESULTS PRODUCED BY
THE UNWISE & REVOLTING CUSTOM OF INHUMING THE DEAD IN
THE MIDST OF THE LIVING.

by G. A. Walker, Surgeon.

——————————AND WHO WOULD LAY
HIS BODY IN THE CITY BURIAL-PLACE,
TO BE THROWN UP AGAIN BY SOME RUDE SEXTON,
AND YIELD ITS NARROW HOUSE ANOTHER TENANT,
ERE THE MOIST FLESH HAD MINGLED WITH THE DUST,
ERE THE TENACIOUS HAIR HAD LEFT THE SCALP,
EXPOSED TO INSULT LEWD, AND WANTONNESS ?
NO, I WILL LAY ME IN THE VILLAGE GROUND;
THERE ARE THE DEAD RESPECTED.

H. K. White.

London
MESSRS LONGMAN & COMPY PATERNOSTER ROW.

Nottingham
J. HICKLIN, PELHAM STREET.
1839.

Entered at Stationers Hall

Engraved by S. Clapp, 111 High Holborn.

PREFACE.

A Work expressly on the Burial Places of the Metropolis is, I believe, a novelty in this country. I entered upon the investigation with much earnestness, because I was convinced that it would open a wide field for interesting and useful suggestions, and although I have experienced interruptions and delays in the prosecution of my undertaking, I am willing to believe that the information communicated will atone for the procrastination of the Work. Burial places in the neighbourhood of the living are, in my opinion, a national evil—the harbingers, if not the originators of pestilence ; the cause, direct or indirect, of inhumanity, immorality, and irreligion. These remarks may appear extravagant and untenable. I have to request an attentive and impartial perusal of the following pages : the proof will be found convincing—the justification complete. The peculiar character and virulence of diseases in the proximity of grave yards first excited my suspicion : evidence, positive and circumstantial, has established the fact—that the miasmata from animal putrescency may occasion not only the instantaneous loss of human existence, but increase the intensity of pestilential diseases.

Every member of society is interested in the statement—that in the Metropolis and in very many towns and villages of the empire, the abodes of the dead are insecure. By far the greater number of grave yards are crowded to excess : many, indeed, have been in this condition for an indefinite period ; so that additional interments could not have taken place without a very questionable disturbance and displacement of previous deposits. The mere allusion to this particular will, I am aware, arouse the sensibilities of our nature ; but the proof is adamantine.

Are these the "consecrated grounds"—the "sanctuaries"—the "resting places" of our ancestors ? Let the inquiry be instituted, by whom are these violations of the grave directed, or sanctioned, or committed—and on what authority ? This is an inquiry which essentially interests all classes of the community ; and, perhaps more than any other, " comes home to men's business and bosoms."

It would seem that interment of the dead within Churches or Vaults, or in Burying Grounds, surrounded with houses, or in the immediate vicinity of densely populated Cities or Towns, is so familiar from its frequent or daily occurrence—accidents *clearly* traceable to the influence of putrefying effluvia so seldom, comparatively, arise from the practice of inhumation—that the most perfect indifference appears to prevail upon the subject; no danger seems to be dreaded, no fear excited, no apprehension even entertained of the injurious and destructive agencies which are constantly in operation, and armed with invisible and irresistible powers. It would not be difficult to shew, that some of the most afflictive visitations of Providence, have originated in the contamination of the atmosphere, from putrefying animal substances—and that to the neighbourhood of the " Grave Yard" may be attributed the violence, if not the origin, of some of the most destructive diseases which have depopulated the human race.

In this Work will be found a comprehensive history of the modes of Interment among all nations, from the remotest antiquity ; shewing that the wisest among mankind, not only perceived the dangers to be apprehended from the burial of the dead in the neighbourhood of the living, but rigidly prohibited the practice. An account is then given of the gradual infringement of the wise restrictions of antiquity—the extent to which the infringement was carried—and the extremely fatal consequences resulting from it. It will be shown, that in countries calling themselves Christian, the revolting practice had alarmingly prevailed, and that Governments could only be brought to legislate upon the subject, from the calamitous and depopulating consequences which were incessantly forcing themselves upon the attention. It will be seen, too, that of those States which had entertained the question, few had attempted to carry out their object by any *efficient* sanatory regulations. France, indeed, stands pre-eminent in this particular. In America, prohibitions have been enforced; and a few minor States have followed in the train;—but England looks on, a silent and unmoved spectatress of some of the most offensive and dangerous encroachments upon the security and sanctity of the " resting places" of her dead.

The nature and effects of the various deleterious products of human putrefaction, are enumerated and explained. The opinions of medical writers and philosophers, and the experiments upon which those opinions were formed, are accurately given. The description and state of some of the Metropolitan Burial Grounds, and the direful consequences attendant on their vicinity to the abodes of man, are correctly and impartially recorded. The abuses of Interment—abuses which afflict while they disgust, are exposed and reprobated; and the whole is concluded by a few General Reflections.

This work, written under the many disadvantages attendant upon the interruptions of extensive and laborious duties, will, notwithstanding, furnish ample materials to exercise the serious consideration of the enlightened Statesman—the profound Philosopher—and the sincere and benevolent Christian: in truth, all men are interested in the weighty matters here discussed. Our best affections are involved, and call upon us to secure, by every contrivance, the peaceful repose of the departed; and, at the same time, to remove as far as possible from the living, THE PESTIFEROUS EXHALATIONS OF THE DEAD.

I may be allowed to state that I am entirely unconnected with any speculation, public or private—having reference to the establishment of Cemeteries, commending the efforts of private individuals, who have originated a reform, which should have commenced with the Executive ;—I am, nevertheless, so fully convinced of the necessity for *legislative interference* to destroy the present dangerous system of inhumation, that I hesitate not to express my opinion, that the *Government* of the country will ultimately be driven to the adoption of means for ENFORCING THE PROHIBITION OF INTERMENT IN THE VICINITY OF THE LIVING.

G. A. WALKER.

101, Drury Lane, London,
November, 1839.

CONTENTS.

Page

CONTENTS.

xiv.   CONTENTS.

Page

ON THE GROSS ABUSES ; THE DANGEROUS, OFFENSIVE, AND DEMORALIZING CONSEQUENCES OF THE PRESENT MODES OF INTERMENT.

ERRATA.

Page 20, last line but 4, read forgot for forget.

32, line 13, read Flaminia for Fluaminia.

48, line 19, read Protais for Prolais.

53, line 27, read adeo for a Deo.

54, line 25, read dicatur for ducatur.

56, line 17, read Erardus for Erasdus.

line 25, read Eod for Evd.

58, line 8, read Joovan for Jivier.

line 28, read Philosophe for Philosopher.

59, line 28, read consuetudine for consuetridine.

105, line 13, read Tissot for Tissol.

117, line 19, read couronne for comonne.

METROPOLITAN
BURYING PLACES.

————"Here's fine revolution, an' we had the trick to see't. Did these bones cost no more the breeding but to play at loggats with them? Mine ache to think on't."—*Hamlet*.

That London, the seat of science, the arena of inventions, the vast amphitheatre where all that is great, good, and noble; all that is conducive to the comforts and the pleasures of life—all that the mind of man can conceive for good or evil—that London, with its thousands of busy minds and observant eyes, anxiously exploring the dimly shadowed outline of the future, yet neglecting the awful monitions of the past ;—should bear upon its breast those plague spots, the BURIAL GROUNDS, must appear to every reflecting mind, an anomaly not easily explained. Yet thus it is—whilst men are daily developing the simple and beautiful laws of the universe, and basing upon them systems as comprehensive as the laws they illustrate—the most perfect indifference is manifested as to the wilful infringement of those laws, and the most con-

B

temptuous disregard of the direful consequences which result from such violations.

This state of things cannot wholly be ascribed to ignorance; for though in this modern Babylon the busy tide of human existence rolls on in its mighty course, there are those who by their scientific attainments, their leisure, and their acknowledged ability, must be supposed attentive to the action of general agencies, and fully cognizant of the evils inseparably connected with the present mode of burying the dead:—there are—there must be, men, who, standing aloof from the passions, the employments, and the anxieties that actuate large communities, have leisure for reflection, and time for execution;—yet *they* have not attempted to rouse the public mind to the consideration of a most important, though latent cause of disease and death:—so important, indeed, do I consider this subject, that I have spared neither time, labour, nor expense in the investigation; and, after mature reflection, I felt I had a stern and inexorable duty to perform; otherwise, I should have shrunk from the task I have undertaken.

Although I consider that a large proportion of those diseases, which are daily prostrating their victims, may be increased, if not generated, by exhalations arising from the putrefaction of dead bodies on the very surface of the earth, I am fully aware, and prepared to admit, that the state of the slaughter houses, and the condition of the sewers in my own and other neighbourhoods—contribute also to propagate or increase disease : the physical condition of the poor, too—the state of many of their habitations (called houses by courtesy)—the narrowness of the lanes or streets in which they reside, excluding too often the rays of the sun, and the free circulation of air, tend materially to increase the evil ; and thus by the artificial barriers built on the authority of the accumulated ignorance, and the heartless cupidity of money-getting men—" the penny wise and pound foolish of their day and generation"—the action of causes constantly producing disease—has alarmingly progressed.

If it be urged that the poor in all communities are, from their circumstances, their condition, their habits, and modes of living, doomed to furnish a greater proportion towards the debt all must pay, I reply, that the genuine philanthrophist will *seek out* objects for the exercise of his charity and beneficence, from among his own countrymen : he will endeavour to lessen the load of misery pressing them, like an incubus, to the earth ; he will, in the exercise of his God-like office, remember that though all mankind are brethren, " Charity beginneth at home." If a moiety of the enormous sums annually sent out of this country for the purposes of religious instruction, were appropriated, under wise management, to the *improvement* of the temporal and spiritual condition of our own too frequently degraded and brutalised poor ; and if *they* could be convinced that many who discourse to them " of righteousness, *temperance,* and judgment to come," cared more for their well being in this life, and evinced their anxiety, by their efforts for the amelioration of the degraded and wretched condition of too large a proportion of their fellow-men—the improvement in society would rapidly advance ; but if the wealthy and the influential, instead of directing the national energies to one of their legitimate objects—the abridgment of the vast mass of human wretchedness in the very centre of the metropolis of the empire,—continue to cultivate and nourish a spurious philanthrophy—if they *will* wait for " a more convenient season," I may be allowed to observe, that the morbid sensibility that descants so feelingly *on transmarine objects of compassion,* cannot have informed itself of the moral and physical condition of too many of our own countrymen, who, like living spectres, or the personifications of hopeless misery, of incurable disease, and too frequently of reckless conduct, are crawling about our streets, spreading contamination around, presenting centres of infection morally and physically in their own persons, and appealing in the most forcible manner to our sympathies—sternly demanding, if they are men, whether we are Christians?

What a magnificent field for exertion is here presented! If, instead of directing the eleemosynary contributions of the middle and lower classes, and the liberal donations of the rich, into foreign channels of usefulness, it were the fashion to irrigate our own soil with that stream, that " quality of mercy that blesseth him that gives, and him that takes," how happy might we not be, how contented our poor, how firm in their affections to those above them in station!—then our women and men (some of the causes of their physical and moral degradation being removed) would become better mothers, better husbands, better members of the family of which they form so large a proportion!

It is demonstrable that the centres of infection are found principally in crowded neighbourhoods, and a vitiated atmosphere; here they are propagated and nourished by the action and re-action, the cause and effect constantly in operation;—for, in many of these very districts, the so-called burying places, the receptacles for the dead, are situated; their insatiable appetite, yet unglutted, is constantly devouring fresh victims, and these again are ejected, after a slight sojourn, to make room for the succeeding occupants, who retain their situation only by the interest or caprice of a hireling grave-digger.

Upon a matter so intimately connected with the prosperity and happiness of a State, the attention of the Government cannot be too anxiously directed. Who will venture to affirm that the *health* of a community is not of the first importance to the stability and prosperity of society? Without health,—riches, honours, and distinctions are comparatively worthless to their possessors.—Who can doubt but that a healthy people are the most valuable defenders of the soil; the most formidable in war, and the most useful in time of peace? Throughout all ages rulers have unfortunately manifested but little regard to the interests or the amelioration of the condition of the poor, and have resisted every attempt at amendment, until by some dreadful calamity they have been driven to measures of improvement.

The atrocities of Burke and Hare exposed the

nefarious practices then carried on to supply the profession with anatomical subjects : these were with difficulty obtained, and large sums of money were demanded, and necessarily paid for them, which operated, not only as obstacles to the improvement of science, but also as premiums for murder ; and it was only the recklessness of perpetration that called forth the interference of the Legislature, and the adoption and enforcement of an efficient remedy. (¹)

The plague, followed by the great fire of London, was succeeded by the improvement, aggrandisement, and splendour of the modern Babylon ; and much yet remains to be done in the way of social improvement, ere the foul blot, cast upon the shield of civilization, be removed.

Medical men, despite of the obstructions thrown in their path, by the varying phenomena offered to their views, as contrasted with the nearly uniform operations presented to the attention of the natural philosopher, often, by analogical reasoning, arrive at

(¹) I shall produce, in another part of this work, evidence of one of the destructive consequences that have resulted from the mistaken act of the Legislature that stigmatised dissection, by directing the bodies of murderers only to be employed for this purpose. I shall demonstrate the existence of a particularly injurious practice which has arisen, I believe, from this remote cause.

conclusions in their own minds that, failing to convince the minds of others, may yet justify their attempt to do so; and, says Dr. Pascalis, an American writer on this subject, "It is the duty of those who by their profession or study, obtain a greater share of knowledge on some points than their fellow citizens may possess, to remonstrate with them against practices that endanger their own safety, or which are contrary to the well-being of the community at large."

Many sources of disease may be pointed out which might be removed. It may be highly instructive to enquire—how much depends upon our own conduct?—how much belongs to the action of those inscrutable causes over which we have no controul? That many of these sources of disease are removable I am certain : would that I could inspire my countrymen *with that active personal benevolence which alone can remove some of the miseries incidental to, and consequent upon, the condition of poverty.* Their noble, their magnificent generosity has never been withheld, even from those who have infinitely less claim upon their sympathies. Would to God that a body, who might be called "legion," would stand forth, and in grappling with the monster, whose gigantic proportions have overshadowed the land, make their determination to accept no compromise, until by a well-considered, well-directed, mighty effort, they have rendered themselves more victorious than the soldier, whose reputation, built on human sacrifices, is too often based upon the number of his victims,—whilst theirs shall be registered in the applause of the good, in the gratitude of millions.

The vast numbers of burying places within the bills of mortality are so many centres or foci of infection—generating constantly the dreadful effluvia of human putrefaction—acting according to the circumstances of locality, nature of soil, depth from the surface, temperature, currents of air—its moisture or dryness, and the power of resistance in those subjected to its influence—(and who is not?) —as a slow or an energetic poison.

The late fatal affair in Aldgate (detailed in another place), elucidates this question. The concentrated energy of a poison, capable of depriving instantly two human beings of life, and periling the life of a third, will be admitted; whilst the reflection will obtrude itself on every thinking person—how long is this state of things to continue? Who is not deeply interested in this question? Families, home, kindred, relations, friends, the thousand sympathies that have grown with our growth and strengthened with our strength,—are so intimately connected with our subject, that the more deeply we reflect, the more settled is our conviction of the necessity for the interference of the Legislature upon a point so intimately involving the best interests of society. I have freely and earnestly spoken of the tremendous risk incurred by the mutilations of the resistless dead, portions of whose bodies, in various stages of decomposition, are thus made the instruments of punishment to the living. Yet no attention is paid to remonstrance, urged from conviction; no heed given to warnings, however disinterested, and however urgent.

I would not unnecessarily alarm the public mind, but the opinions I have advanced are not hypothetical; they are founded upon the experience and practices of past ages, and confirmed by the experience and practice of the present day: and, therefore, as this momentous subject has hitherto, "*mirabile dictu!*" been passed over in total silence, as though insignificant or indifferent, by *English* writers of eminence, I have not hesitated, feeling the *paramount* importance of the question, to throw my mite into the public treasury, hoping to see, at least, as the result of my labours, the enforcement of efficient " Sanatory Regulations" throughout every department of the kingdom, and the ENTIRE REMOVAL OF THE DEAD FROM THE IMMEDIATE PROXIMITY OF THE LIVING. "The necessity of removing burial places to a distance from the habitations of men, has been felt by all nations in every age. It is founded upon the dangers which arise from the exhalations of animal decomposition."

A very full detail will be given in a subsequent part of this work of the dangers arising from the decomposition of putrifying animal matter, and the diseases generated by it. The following extracts will not fail to stimulate the *awakening anxieties* of the most sceptical of my readers;—the first is taken from the Cyclopœd. of Prac. Medicine, p. 356, art. Plague: and the other is an extract from a "Tour through Germany, by the Rev. Dr. Render," inserted in the American Gazette of Health, No. 1, p. 2 :—

" An American merchant ship was lying at anchor in Wampoa Roads, 16 miles from Canton. One of her crew died of dysentery. He was taken on shore to be buried. No disease of any kind had occured in the ship from her departure from America, till her arrival in the river Tigris. Four men accompanied the corpse, and two of them began to dig a grave. Unfortunately, they began in a spot where a human body had been buried about two or three months previously. The instant the spade went through the lid of the coffin, a most dreadful effluvium issued forth, and the two men fell down nearly lifeless. It was with the greatest difficulty their companions could approach near enough to drag them from the spot, and fill up the place with earth. The two men then recovered a little, and with assistance reached the boat and returned on board. On the succeeding morning, they presented the following symptoms : very acute head-ache, with a sense of giddiness and dimness of sight (which had existed more or less from the moment of opening the grave) ; eyes of a peculiar muddy appearance ; oppression about the præcordia ; dull heavy pain in the regions of the heart and liver, with slight palpitation at times, and fluttering pulse ; sense of extreme debility, with occasional convulsive or spasmodic twitchings of the muscles of the lower extremities ; nausea ; slight diarrhœa ; rigors, succeeded by flushings of the face, neck, breast, and upper extremities ; tongue white and much loaded ; pulse from 110 to 120, weak and irregular ; urine scanty and high-coloured, and skin sometimes dry, sometimes covered with a clammy sweat. On the fourth day from the commencement of the attack, numerous petechiæ appeared over the breast and arms, and in one of the patients, a large bubo formed in the right groin, and another in the axilla of the same side, which speedily ran to suppuration. To one, the disease proved fatal on the evening of the fourth day; to the other, on the morning of the fifth.

" One of the two men, not immediately engaged in digging the grave, was attacked on the eighth day from his being on shore. The symptoms resembled those in the preceding cases. For three days previously to the avowed attack of illness, there had been pain and enlargement of one of the inguinal glands, which at the period he was visited, had acquired the size of a hen's egg ; and early in the disease, the breast and arms were covered with petechiæ. By active treatment this person recovered, as likewise did the fourth man, who had slight indisposition of no decided character."

───────────

" How pernicious the burying in churches is to a congregation, will appear from the following serious instance of the consequences resulting from it :—

" My readers will, I hope, permit me to suppress the real names of the clergyman, and the place where this event took place.

" In the month of July, 17—, a very corpulent lady died at ——. Before her death, she begged as a particular favour, to be buried in the parochial church. She had died on the Wednesday, and on the following Saturday was buried, according to her desire. The weather at the time was very hot, and a great drought had prevailed. The succeeding Sunday, a week after the lady had been buried, the Protestant clergyman had a very full congregation, upwards of nine hundred persons attending, that being the day for administering the Holy Sacrament. It is the custom in Germany, that when people wish to receive the Sacrament, they neither eat nor drink until the ceremony is over. The clergyman consecrates the bread and wine, which is uncovered during the ceremony. There were about one hundred and eighty communicants. A quarter of an hour after the ceremony, before they had quitted the church, more than sixty of the communicants were taken ill : several died in the most violent agonies ; others of a more vigorous constitution survived by the help of medical assistance ; a most violent consternation prevailed among the whole congregation, and throughout the town, and it was concluded that the wine had been poisoned. The Sacristan, and several others belonging to the vestry, were put in irons. The persons arrested underwent very great hardships : during the space of a week they were confined in a dungeon, and some of them were put to the torture ; but they persisted in their innocence.

" On the Sunday following, the magistrate ordered that a chalice of wine, uncovered, should be placed for the space of an hour, upon the altar : the hour had scarcely elapsed, when they beheld the wine filled with myriads of insects—by tracing whence they came, it was perceived, by the rays of the sun, that they issued from the grave of the lady who had been buried the preceding fortnight. The people not belonging to the vestry were dismissed, and four men were employed to open the vault and the coffin ; in doing this, two of them dropped down and expired on the spot, the other two were only saved by the utmost exertions of medical talent. It is beyond the power of words to describe the horrid appearance of the corpse when the body was opened. The whole was an entire mass of putrefaction ; and it was now clearly perceived that the numerous insects, together with the effluvia which had issued from the body, had caused the pestilential infection, which was a week before attributed to poison. It is but justice to add, that on this discovery, the accused persons were liberated, and every atonement made by the magistrates and clergyman for their misguided conduct."—(*New York Gazette of Health*, No. 1, p. 2.)

A comprehensive sketch of the modes of interment among different nations, and in different periods, may not be unacceptable to my readers. Professor Scipione Piattoli, in his work " on the Dangers of Interment," published in 1774, treated this branch of the subject with considerable ability. M. Vicq. d'Azyr, Regent of the Faculty of Medicine of Paris, translated the work of the Italian into the French language, and enriched it with valuable notes. I am indebted to that translation for the following HISTORICAL SUMMARY.

HISTORY

OF THE

BURIAL PLACES AMONG THE ANCIENTS.

It is not necessary, nor would it be useful, to detail the unsatisfactory opinions and statements of many writers, as to the superstitions and absurd customs relative to the interment or distribution of the dead, among nations scarcely civilized, or among the most barbarous tribes. We are informed, that some Indians feasted on the slain, and murdered and devoured the sick and the aged—that some exposed their dead, to be devoured by wild beasts—that others cast their dead into rivers and ponds, and that the Scythians buried them in snow, or burned them to cinders. Undoubtedly, the most ancient and the most common practice, was to bury the dead in the ground; for, " it appeared just to restore human bodies to the common mother from which they sprung." (¹) Some instances were found

(¹) It would be tedious to point out how much the customs of different nations have varied upon the subject of burials. We may judge of them, by the following description, extracted from Spondanus.—(*Cœmet. sacra, p.* 20, 21.) According to this author, the Syrcanians abandoned their dead to the dogs; some Indians left them to the vultures; the Garamantians covered them with sand; and the Celts, by a singular caprice, took from them the bony

of men deeply affected with grief, who surmounting the horror which a dead body excites, endured the presence of it for some time; either hoping it would return to life, or thinking it impossible to separate themselves altogether from it; (^{1}) thus they sought to derive consolation for the loss they had recently sustained. The voice of religion, of nature, and of policy, however, engaged men to hasten the burial of their dead.

cap of the cranium for cups, which they set in gold. The Ethiopians, and the greatest part of the Ictytophages, threw their dead into the water, willing to give back to the fish the food derived from them. The inhabitants of Colchis, and the Phrygians, hung them on trees, to present to the air a part of the aliment it had furnished. The Egyptians embalmed their dead; the Persians enveloped theirs in wax; and the Babylonians and Syrians preserved their dead in honey. The Lacedemonians and Scythians embalmed their kings also in honey. The Islanders of Delos buried their dead in the neighbouring islands. The Megarians, in the Island of Salamis; the Greeks and Romans destroyed their dead by fire; the bodies of infants, however, were excepted, for it was feared, says Pliny, that their teeth would be consumed; and, according to the opinion of these nations, the teeth contained the principle of the resurrection; and many Jewish Rabbi yet believe, that there is a bone in the skeleton called *Luz*, which they place in the spinal column, and believe it to be indestructible.— *(Diemerbroek, Treatise on Anatomy.)*

(^{1}) In remote antiquity, so high a value was placed upon the preservation of these precious relics, that the privation of them was considered as the most afflicting and exemplary punishment. Thus Asychis, king of Egypt, wishing to compel his subjects to pay his debts, ordered them to furnish, as pledges, the urns which contained the ashes of their ancestors; adding, that those who did not perform their engagements, should be deprived of the honours of sepulchre.—*(Spond. p. 367.)*

The Egyptians attached a flattering idea of honour to the tomb—they considered it a recompense for virtue, and a public object of emulation. The severe examination which followed upon the death of a citizen—the sombre lake destined to decide upon the character which each should hold in the estimation of posterity,—furnished interesting motives to all, upon the subject of interment. (¹) Religion, also, bringing with it the consoling doctrine of a future life, in which the soul would preserve some recollection of past existence, excited respect for the tombs of those who had lived well. It was a crime to disturb the remains of the dead in their asylum; a noble desire of obtaining funeral honours influenced every heart; a veneration for tombs thus became a part of religious worship. To render promptly the last duties to the dead, was from that moment a sacred obligation. Whoever left a dead body on the road, without covering it with earth, was guilty of monstrous impiety. To break open tombs—to scatter here and there the unburied

(¹) The Egyptians were subjected, after death, to a public examination, upon the borders of the marshy lake, Acheron, whither they were carried for that purpose. The bodies of virtuous and worthy citizens were placed, by order of the Judges, in a bark, which transported them to the other side of the lake, where public tombs were erected in a delightful country. Those deemed unworthy were deprived of this honour; they were thrown, probably, into a loathsome pit, which took the name of *Tartarus*, from the use to which it was destined. This gave rise to the fables of the river Lethe—of the boatman Charon—the three Judges of Hell—and the wandering of a hundred years upon the borders of the Styx.—(*Diod. Sic.* l. 7.)

C

bones, was horrible sacrilege. Whoever touched a body before it had received the honours of sepulchre, was guilty of a profanation which the lustral waters alone could wash away. In some other places, a person rendered himself impure, by only walking over a place where a body was interred. Acting upon these impressions, a little modified, they would neither build houses nor erect walls; nor, by any means, construct temples, on grounds which had been used for inhumation : a precaution which tended evidently to separate, as far as possible, the dead from the living, and to fix sepulchres in distant situations.

The Germans, who possessed large forests, burned their dead. Homer says the same thing of the Phrygians, and Virgil of the Trojans. Inhumation, however, was not forbidden; and we find among them many instances of it. The respect which the Persians had for the sun and for fire, induced them to consider the burning of the dead as criminal.

The Assyrians, Medes, Parthians, Tyrians, Phœnicians, Ethiopians, the Egyptians themselves, and the Persians had always vaults for their dead, and places particularly destined for them. The Chinese and the Peruvians, situated on the opposite extremities of the earth, had the same practice in this respect. The tombs of Kings, and of great men of the most remote antiquity, were in caverns, carefully made in the midst of the most solitary mountains. Gyges, king of Lydia, was buried at the foot of Mount Tmolus. The Kings of Persia had their sepulchres on the Royal Mountain, near the city of Persepolis; Sylvius Aventinus was buried on the hill that bears his name, and King Dercennus within a high mountain, as Virgil attests.—(Æneid, l. 11, 850.)

The ancient Russians transported the dead bodies of their Princes to the deep caverns along the Boristhenes; travellers who are curious, yet visit them daily. The Danes constructed artificial mountains, to entomb in them the bodies of their Kings.

The loss of a beloved object required some reparation—hence the idea of pencilling the outline and preserving the portrait. This desire, although indifferent in itself to the well being of society, has, however, been turned to its advantage. But man, guided by his passions, is easily carried by them beyond the bounds of reason; instead of portraits, busts, and prints, men wished to keep the bodies themselves. The restless grief of a father, a son, a widow, or a lover, invented the art, till then unknown, of giving a kind of life to inanimate bodies. The Egyptians, from whom other nations have learned whatever polishes and softens the manners, invented the art of *embalming* the dead, and rendering it innoxious to the living. Self love gave additional force to this invention, which was afterwards universally adopted and practised. It was thought that the soul remained hovering around the body as long as it preserved its form entire and intact. This opinion, at first, gave great importance to the art of embalming; but the dangerous consequences of it were soon so evident, that the public authorities first censured, and ultimately abolished it.([1]) This superstitious practice was prevalent only among the great and the wealthy.([2]) The common people, that is the greatest number, in all nations, were always contented with the inhumation of the body; there have even been whole

([1]) Many facts demonstrate that attempts were made to reconcile funeral ceremonies with the opinions of philosophy. Herodotus wished bodies to be burned, that they might the more quickly return to their constituent principles. Thales, the Milesian, who recognized no other principle than water, contended for inhumation; for, according to his system, the bosom of the earth contained dissolvents capable of reducing a body to its first principles. The disciples of Pythagoras, full of mysterious ideas of the nature of plants and legumes, covered dead bodies with the leaves of aloes and of poplar. The Cynics and Pyrrhonians, were indifferent upon this point.

([2]) Every thing believed to be impure was removed from this ceremony. Woollen stuffs were prohibited—linen only was used. Small statues of marble, of copper, or of clay, which represented Osiris or Pluto, Isis or Proserpine, were found in bodies embalmed. Large sums of money, or very valuable articles were enclosed in the tombs. The Spaniards found, in the West Indies, tombs filled with gold and other articles of great value. The Jews buried immense treasures with their dead. Plutarch and Strabo relate that the Kings of Persia and Macedonia ordered their treasures to be enclosed in their tombs : this practice was also very frequent among the Romans; it is of the highest antiquity. The ancient Pagans never forget to put a piece of money into the mouths of the defunct, which they designated by the name of *Obolum* or *Trientem.* Virgil, speaking of the dead, often calls them *inopem turbam.—(Spond. p.* 59, 61, 70, and 111.)

nations among whom inhumation was generally and uninterruptedly practised.

Contagious diseases had more than once shown the necessity of removing the dead to a distance from the habitations of the living. The great number of dead bodies, after a sanguinary battle, compelled the survivors to burn them, and to preserve their ashes. These means were judiciously employed to destroy the custom of *embalming*, then too much extended ; and they succeeded so much the better, as they were not opposed to the prevailing opinions. In a short time, the whole face of things was changed, and tombs and urns were filled with the ashes of the dead. The custom of burning the dead extended even among people, who till then, had practised simple inhumation. It was observed that long wars, frequent transmigrations, the destruction and rebuilding of cities, might, with the revolution of times, overturn the whole surface of a country; and that bones, confided for several centuries to the bosom of the earth, would then unavoidably be exposed upon the surface. The fear of such a profanation determined the practice of burning the dead—their repose, from that moment, was considered as secure.

They went still further : they excluded from the walls and precincts of cities these ashes, which they ever regarded, however, with respect; and the places which had been consecrated for ordinary burials, were destined to receive the urns. The highways were for a long time bordered with tombs, and with grave-stones, covered with inscriptions. Thus the passer-by was readily instructed in the glorious actions of his ancestors; and every one found there examples for conduct, and subjects for emulation. A glance over the remains of great men made every one feel his own weakness. Carnage, fire, and destruction were thus also kept at a distance from the cities; the people being compelled to leave their walls to defend these sacred deposits; it would have been criminal to abandon them as a prey to the enemy.

Religion introduced new dogmas which favoured this custom. Philosophy adopted different opinions upon the nature of spirits, and the activity of fire: it was thought that bodies were thus promptly restored to their original principles; the soul, it was said, "readily disengaged from its prison, purified by fire, and delivered from the burden of a perishable body, is rapidly attracted towards its own sphere, and presses on to unite itself with the soul of the universe." The Egyptians adopted this opinion, and their industry found out the means of preserving the ashes of their dead, in the incombustible amianthus. We may presume, from the great expense attendant upon the funeral pile, and the aromatics employed, that the common people never obtained that distinction.

If we examine history, we shall find that soldiers were at all times employed in the construction of roads; and that they always made subterranean cavities at a distance from cities. It is equally certain that, in several countries, public funds were assigned for the construction of tombs, as well as for the maintenance of funeral piles; which were almost always burning in extensively populated States.

In the midst of so many customs which caprice and vanity produced in different states, the influence of nature, of laws, and of religion, was always exerted to separate the dead from the living; and the end for which tombs had been constructed at a distance from cities was always kept in view.

We will now take a transient view of the funeral ceremonies of the Jews, the Greeks, and the Romans; we shall find in them the elements of our own customs.

SEPULCHRES AMONG THE JEWS.

The first foundations of Christianity were laid among the Jews; and the primitive Church was formed of proselytes from Greece and Latium. The traces of Judaic antiquity, always preserved inviolable and pure, lead us back to the most ancient times, in which inhumation was generally practised. A dreadful crime brought death into the world: Cain, after having killed his brother, thought to conceal his crime by covering the body with earth; after this dreadful example they continued to *inhume* the bodies of the dead in open deserts and uninhabited places. The ridiculous traditions of the Rabbis, adopted by some of our historians, have accredited the fable of the bones and scull of our first father, which they pretend were scrupulously preserved by Noah until the deluge. Abraham bought from the children of Heth, the Cave of Hebron, where he deposited the corpse of Sarah. He himself was buried there; and after him Isaac, Rebecca, and Leah. The tomb of Rachel was placed along the road from Jerusalem to Ephrata. Jacob likewise purchased from the children of Shechem a piece of ground, where he had a tomb erected. He was buried there with much pomp, by his son Joseph, who had him brought from Egypt, where he died. Joseph and all his brethren were buried in the same place. (¹) During the Egyptian captivity, the tombs of the Israelites were undoubtedly made in some distant place, according to the custom of the people in whose country they were fixed. Their long wanderings in the desert served also to establish this custom. Moses was buried by the order of God himself, in the Valley of Moab; Miriam, his sister, at Kadesh; Aaron, at Hor; and Eleazar, the son of the latter, as well as Joshua, on the mountains of Ephraim. After the entry of the Jews into the promised land, the establishment of the Jewish law, and the inauguration of religious ceremonies, it was acknowledged that the commands

(¹) It is believed, as commentators say, that the remains of all these illustrious patriarchs, of whom we have just spoken, were collected in the Cave of Hebron, with the bones of Abraham.—(*Vide* CALMET, *ad Act. Apost. c.* 7—36, *and ibid.*)

of God were opposed to the dangerous vicinity of the dead. According to their customs, the touch of a dead body contracted a legal impurity; to efface which, the clothes were to be washed. To bury the dead in the houses of individuals, was to render them unclean. This regulation made them attentive to remove the dead from their dwellings. They dreaded all communication with them, so much so that travellers were even forbidden to walk upon places where the dead were buried, and which were distinguished by the erection of small pillars. They took great care to paint the outside of their tombs white, which they renewed every year. They were permitted, however, to have their sepulchres at their country residences; and there, in full splendour, was exhibited the luxury of the great and of the heads of the nation. The nurse of Rebecca and Deborah was buried at the foot of a tree. The unfortunate Saul had the same fate. (¹) The priests were buried on their own estates, and sometimes in the tombs of kings. (²) Vaults, dug on Mount Zion, under the foundations of the Temple, and in the royal gardens, were destined for the sepulchres of the Kings of Judah. No remarkable change in this particular afterwards occurred, notwithstanding the eventful vicissitudes this nation experienced. If

(¹) He was buried under a tree, near Jabesh Gilead.—(1 *Sam.* c. 31, *v.* 13.) From thence David carried his remains, or his bones, burnt to ashes, to the sepulchre of Kish, the father of Saul, in the territory of Benjamin.—(2 *Sam.* c. 21, *v.* 12.)

(*) II. Paralip. 24, 16.

we judge by some passages of scripture, it appears that a few foreign customs only, such as burning the dead,([1]) and embalming them, were introduced among them. In Paralipomenes, and the books of Jeremiah, mention is made of the ceremony of burning the dead, as a rite introduced in favour of Kings. ([2]) Perhaps this custom was of short duration, and peculiar only to a few. The bodies of Saul and Jonathan were burnt to ashes, by the people of Jabesh Gilead, to protect them from the fury of the Philistines. ([3])

Thus we see that caverns and fields have always been destined for places of burial. ([4]) Elijah was inhumed in a grotto, where other bodies also were placed, among which was one that, according to the Holy Scriptures, miraculously recovered life by touching the prophet. Lazarus was buried at Bethany—Joseph of Arimathea, a man of importance among the Jews, had a tomb hewn out of a rock in a garden, near to Golgotha, the place of the sepulchre of Jesus Christ. Many holy persons who were

([1]) According to Spondanus (*Cæmet. sacra, p.* 158), the Hebrews burned perfumes upon the dead, which they called *combustion,* whence, as he says, it has been erroneously concluded that they were accustomed to burn dead bodies also.

([2]) A continual fire, that consumed the dead, and other filth of the city, burned perpetually in the deep ditch of Topheth, which was in the Valley of Hinnon.—(*Isaiah, c.* 30, *v.* 33.) This tradition has furnished the name and the idea of what is called *geenna* or *gehenna.*—(CALMET *Dict. Bibl. art. Cedron.)*

([3]) Necessity at this moment obliged them to adopt this course.

([4]) CALMET *Dict. Bibl. art. Sepulchrum.*

resuscitated, at the death of our Saviour, were entombed out of Jerusalem, for it is written in the Scriptures, that immediately after they had been restored to life, they returned into that city.

Every city always had its public cemetery out of the walls. Some think that that of Jerusalem was in the valley of Cedron, near which the Pharisees bought the Potter's Field, as a burying ground for strangers. A custom so constant, among a people who had received it from God, and who always very strictly observed it, ought to be considered as a paramount authority among Christians.

FUNERAL RITES OF THE GREEKS.

The most ancient custom among the Greeks was inhumation. The custom of burning the dead, was introduced among them, at a subsequent period. ([1]) The urns, containing the ashes of the dead, were kept in private houses, in the interior of cities, and sometimes even in temples. These examples were, at first, of rare occurrence : and this distinction was only granted to the heads of the government, and to generals who had saved their country. Inhuma-

([1]) Some carry back the origin of this custom to the time of Hercules, who wished to carry, to King Licinius, the sad remains of his son, Argivus, killed in battle.—(*Hom. scoliast. Iliad* 7.) Most think that this custom takes its date from the Trojan war, where the atrocious carnage, and the example of the Phrygians, determined the Greeks to adopt this plan, as the most simple.— (*Vide Potter Archæology,* l. 4. c. 6.)

tion was always more general in Greece, than else-where, and the very salutary custom of conveying the dead to a distance from cities, was inviolably preserved. The Thebans, the people of Sicyon, of Delos and of Megara, the Macedonians, the inhabitants of the Chersonese, and of almost all Greece, adopted the same custom in this respect. (¹) The most celebrated legislators made it an interesting point in their code. Cecrops, at Athens, wished the dead to be carried beyond the walls. Solon adopted and re-established this wise regulation in all its vigour; and it was only during the last days of the republic, at Athens, that a small number of persons were inhumed in the interior of the city. This honourable distinction was only permitted in favour of some heroes. It was thus that they left in the Ceramicus, the tombs of those brave citizens, who sacrificed themselves for the defence of their country. (²) Plato, in his republic, did not even permit inhumation in fields fit for tillage; he reserved for that purpose, dry and sandy grounds, and those which could be employed for no other use.

(¹) Lycurgus was the only one who permitted tombs to be placed in cities, in temples, and in public places, where the people met. He wished to accustom the Spartan youth to bravery and courage, by familiarising them with the idea of death. It seems that he might have accomplished the same end, by following, in respect to funeral rites, the customs adopted by the rest of Greece. —(*Vide Instit. Polit. book* 1, *c.* 1, § 13.)

(²) Towards the latter period of the government of Athens, Sophocles found no tombs in that city; although it was besieged by the Spartans; and Sulpittius, at a less remote period, could not obtain there a sepulchre for Marcellus.

The same laws were in force in *Grecia Magna*. The Carthaginians found the tombs of the inhabitants of Syracuse outside the city. The same thing occurred at Agrigentum. (¹) Religion gave its sanction to this custom. (²) The holiness of tombs, many of which became the temples of certain Divinities, and were regarded as asylums for the unfortunate and the accused—the respect paid to the ashes and the memory of their ancestors—the

(¹) The Tarentines followed the same customs. On one occasion, they consulted the Oracle, and received from it the answer, that they would be much happier, *si cum pluribus habitarent.*—(Polyb. l. 8.) The true sense of the Oracle was, that they should employ means to increase the population. What was their conduct? They allowed the dead to be buried within their walls; and thought they had thus fulfilled the intention of the Oracle. It must be confessed, that this was a strange mode of increasing their population.

(²) No nation was ever more jealous than the Greeks, of paying funeral honours to the dead. The Athenians frequently neglected the advantages of the most illustrious victories, to perform this duty. They often, indeed, notwithstanding these victories, sacrificed excellent generals, because they had not shewn themselves sufficiently zealous in burying the soldiers slain in battle. Those who violated tombs, were considered as victims, irrevocably destined to the anger of the gods. The auguries they derived, the prayers and the vows which they made, over tombs, demonstrate with what earnestness the depositaries of the precepts of religion had recommended the duty of sepulchre. The Greek writers, and especially the poets, have left some interesting details upon this subject.—*(Vide Anthol. and Brodæus Epigr. gr.)* It may be added, that the most solemn oaths, pronounced over tombs, were as sacred as if they had been made over altars. Every one knows that Alexander, before undertaking the Asiatic war, sacrificed upon the tomb of Achilles.

punishments with which their holy laws threatened the violators of these customs—the maledictions denounced upon them by the priests:—in one word, the whole religious doctrine and mythology of the Greeks, tended only to support the laws, which directed the bodies of the dead to be removed far from the habitations of the living.

THE FUNERAL RITES OF THE ROMANS.

The Romans preserved the custom indicated by nature, that of *inhuming* their dead, although they had the right of erecting tombs in their country residences.

Numa was buried upon Mount Janiculum, which was not then within the city. The Kings, who succeeded him, had their sepulchres in the *Campus Martius*, between the city and the Tiber. The vestal virgins enjoyed the privilege of burial within the city—those who had violated the vow of chastity, to which they had pledged themselves, were buried alive, in a field called *Campus Sceleratus*.

The law of the Twelve Tables expressly forbids the burning or burial of any dead body in the city. By the terms even of the law, " Hominem mortuum in urbe ne sepelito neve urito," it clearly appears, that from the fourth century of the republic, they adopted, indifferently, the custom of burning and inhumation.

In the obstinate wars carried on by the Romans

against the barbarians, bones, which had been buried, were frequently seen to be outraged and exposed. The horror excited by religious feelings at such profanations, and the wisdom of the magistrates, united to encourage the burning of the dead. ([1]) It was the means of preventing the evils which the martial genius and superstition of the people were calculated to produce.

It was ordered by their laws, to respect the dead; their asylum was inviolable, and their sepulchre was sacred. ([2]) Religious scruples, upon this point, were carried so far that, not contented with respect for the tombs, the Romans required that the places also destined for sepulchre, should be held particularly sacred.

Under the consulate of Duillius, the most illustrious houses had tombs for their family, in their

([1]) Many of the most illustrious families of Rome did not adopt this new custom. The Cornelian family, for example, continued to bury their dead, until the time of Scylla: he was the first of his family, who ordered that his body should be burned. Historians observe, that he did this, from the fear that his body would be dug up, as he had disinterred that of Marius.—*(Cic.* 2, *de Leg.* 5, *Varr.* 4, *de LL. ubi Scalig. et Turneb.)*

([2]) The respect which the Romans entertained for the sepulchre cannot be questioned. The ceremonies by which these monuments were consecrated to the manes, the punishments denounced against those who stole any thing in these sacred places, and the regulations enforced for the preservation of cleanliness and order, furnish abundant proofs of popular anxiety. An inhumed body could not be removed to another situation, without the consent of the priests; or, in the provinces, without the permission of the magistrates.—*(Hein. Ant. Rom.)*

own grounds, which daily became more enlarged. The lands, however, produced nothing, for want of culture, and the extent of cultivated grounds greatly diminishing, the magistrates felt it to be their duty strenuously to oppose the further increase of the evil. Sepulchres were no longer made in fields. The sepulchres of the most illustrious families, as those of the Metelli, the Claudii, the Scipiones, the Servilii, and the Valerii, were removed, and placed along the highways; and thus contributed to the embellishment of the city.

This wise ordinance gave names to the public ways, as the Via Aurelia, V. Fluaminia, V. Lucilia, V. Appia, V. Laviniana, V. Julia, &c. Many, however, placed their tombs upon the *Collis Hortulorum*, a little above the *Campus Martius*. Religion, which had no other interest upon this point than that of the republic, adopted as of itself, this new arrangement. (¹) The people also had

(¹) Shortly afterwards, the same reason caused the law of the Twelve Tables to be renewed against the custom of interring in cities, which, under the pretext of protecting sepulchres from all profanation, would have infected the places of assembly: *quod iniquum esse putarent locum publicum privatâ religione obligari.*—(*Cic. de Leg.* l. 2.)

On other occasions policy, unprotected by Religion, was compelled to acknowledge its empire. Elien relates that this doctrine served for a specious pretext to the patricians to reject the Agrarian Law proposed by the Gracchi. It was thought to be contrary to good order, that the place in which the ashes of the dead reposed, should thus change masters, and this reflection presented an insurmountable obstacle to the division of lands.—(ELIEN, *var. Hist. l. 2.)*

funeral piles, and common sepulchres. (¹) Some rich citizens, with the view of ingratiating themselves with the people, gave them grounds for common sepulchres. The tombs and funeral rites of great men were paid for out of the funds of the republic, and poor citizens obtained the same favour from the liberality of the Pontiffs.

There were, however, some exceptions in favour of particular individuals. The vestal virgins never lost the privilege of burial within the walls; generals who had received the honours of triumph, possessed the same right; the priests, and afterwards, the ministers of public worship equally enjoyed it. Such a distinction was flattering to self-love; from that time it was generally sought after. Some of the Cæsars, however, were buried out of the walls of Rome. Domitian, in the *Via Latina*; Septimus Severus, in the *Via Appiana*; and another Emperor, in the *Via Laviniana*.

This soon ceased to be considered a privilege; it was either granted too easily, or it was invaded

(¹) *Hoc miseræ plebi stabat commune sepulchrum.—(Horat. l. 1, sat. 8.)*

Such were the small wells *(puticuli)* mentioned in history. Whether they were deep cavities, like wells, or whether this name was given to them from the offensive smell they diffused around, it is certain that these places were cavities into which were thrown the dead bodies of the common people. The places in which they burned the dead were called *ustrinæ*. The small pits were situated upon the Esquiline Hill. There Mecænas had his sepulchre after all the small tombs had been taken away. Horace also had his near that of his friend, whom he had so highly lauded.

D

during the frequent revolutions which the city of Rome experienced. The Emperor Adrian was compelled to prohibit, anew, inhumation in cities; by accident he did not mention the capitals: but Antoninus Pius, in his rescript, included the cities and suburbs of his vast empire. ([1]) The practice of burning the dead was less common under this Emperor; ([2]) it became still less so under his successors; and ceased altogether under the Emperor Gratianus. ([3])

FUNERAL RITES OF THE EARLY CHRISTIANS.

The three nations who composed the primitive church found inhumation established among them by the dogmas of their religion and the laws of their country. The custom of burning their dead was confined to the great and the rich. Burial out of cities was an obligation upon all: if there were any exceptions they were but few in number, and they

([1]) *Vide* the Commentary of Godefroy upon the Code Theodos. l. 9, tit. 17, c. 6; and in the same place, the controversies of learned civilians upon the two laws just mentioned.

([2]) It appears that the practice of embalming also ceased at this period.

([3]) Godefroy, *loc. cit.* thinks this custom was practised under the reign of Theodosius. Macrobius, l. 7, c. 7, asserts, that in his time there was no evidence in its favour. *Licet urendi corpora defunctorum usus nostro tempore nullus fit.* This induces us to believe that the custom of burning the dead did not cease altogether until about the end of the third or fourth century.

were never granted to the common people, nor those who died in private retirement.

The most unjust and unmerited contempt having been the first portion of that holy and admirable religion, which in its rapid and miraculous progress has since enlightened the whole earth, (¹) the burial of

(¹) Those who had expired during punishment for any crime were, by the Roman laws, deprived of sepulchre. The place from which their body was thrown, after having been dragged there, was called *Scalæ Gemoniæ*, and was considered as infamous. (*L.* 48,*ff. tit.* 24, *de Cadav. Punit.*) The political and religious system of the Greeks, also, must have led them to consider the privation of burial as the extreme of misery.—(*Vide Homer Odyss. v.* 66.)

To wish that any one might be deprived of sepulchre was, with them, the most dreadful imprecation. This privation was also the greatest punishment to the criminal; deserters, and persons guilty of sacrilege were of this number.—(*Potter, Archæolog. Grec. l.* 4, *c.* 1.)

Among the Grecians and Romans this was considered so sacred a duty that, after a battle, they were careful to inter the dead even of their enemies; and when generals wished to encourage their soldiers, they promised them the honours of sepulchre.

The respect which the Egyptians had for the tomb, furnished them with a means of vengeance against their enemies. The most outrageous insult they could inflict was to exhume their dead, and beat them with rods.—(*Sp. p.* 450.)

The customs of the Jews differed: no crime among them, in the ordinary course of their law, could deprive the culprit of burial. They sometimes inflicted this severe punishment upon the *uncircumcised*, the irreconcileable enemies of the Jews. Joshua threw into the Cave of Makkedah five Kings, tied together.—(*Jos.* 10, 24.) Joram, Jezebel, and Joachim, were deprived of sepulchre by the order of God.—(2 *Kings*, 9, 24.) It was to them the greatest punishment.—(*Jer.* 8, 2. *Eccl.* 6, 3.) Some authors affirm that the Valley of Tophet was, among the Jews, what the *Scalæ Gemoniæ* was among the Romans.

the first Christians was, at first, that of the people, or that of individuals the least distinguished. When they became a distinct and recognized body, they had their own particular funeral ceremonies, which were derived, partly from the Jews, and partly from the Gentiles. Inhumation was thus established among the Christians: it was the only practice of the Jews whose laws served them for a rule upon all points which were not the object of a particular sanction or belief. If to these considerations, we add the small number of believers, their extreme poverty, the fear they had of the Jews, and their decided aversion for everything which might resemble Paganism, (¹) we shall easily believe, as we have already stated, that the burial of the Christians was that of the common people, of whom they formed part.

Ananias, mentioned in the Acts of the Apostles, expired at the feet of St. Peter: some Christians carried away his body, and put it in the earth; near it, they placed the body of Sapphira, his wife. The Deacon, Stephen, was carefully interred by the Christians, who sprinkled his tomb with their tears. These two burials are mentioned, but the places in which they were made are not specified. (²)

(¹) Tertullian gives another reason, which is satisfactory to some persons. It was believed that the soul still remained after death near the body of him whom it had animated, or that a portion of it, at least, remained there; and they considered it a duty to take care of these precious remains. *Propterea nec ignibus funerandum aiunt, parcentes superfluo animæ.—(De An.* 51.)

(²) It is probable, according to the text of St. Luke, that he was buried in the place where he was stoned, that is to say, out of the city.

However, the persecutions which the Christians had to suffer in the Roman empire, the cruel carnage, of which the barbarous Nero had given the example, and which was so often followed, increased the number of martyrs : the faithful were surrounded by a prodigious number of the dead, exposed to the contempt and the insults of the Pagans.

Gratitude and the tenderest attachment combined with the voice of nature and religion. The Christians determined to seek for these bodies, in order to remove them from the fury of an irritated people; they concealed them at first in the houses of individuals, to transport them afterwards to the public cemeteries, under cover of the night. The most mysterious privacy, the most attentive guard were necessary on this occasion. The catacombs, which some have perhaps improperly confounded with the *puteoli* of the ancient Romans, appeared well suited to secure the repose of these venerable remains. (¹)

The Christians frequently assembled in these dark retreats to celebrate their mysteries. The horror of these places, the black darkness which there prevailed, caused St. Jerome to say, that they

(¹) Pomponius Festus speaks of them *de interpretati.* The catacombs were subterranean excavations, in the neighbourhood of Rome, to be used, according to some, for the sepulchre of the Pagans, who afterwards abandoned the use of them. This word is derived from the Greek ; it signifies a place dug deep. We must not confound the catacombs with the cemeteries ; each of these words has its own signification, and the most celebrated ecclesiastical writers have always distinguished them.

presented to his eyes the image of hell. (¹) Every thing contributed to render equally respectable the place of burial and the funeral ceremonies of the first Christians. The august ceremonies with which these faithful men worshipped the Creator, the participation of the holy sacrament, which was offered in these places, a holy and irreproachable conduct so common in these ages of ardent devotion, procured for the Christians the highest respect. Moreover, they always reserved particular places for the ashes of martyrs, and of those who died in the odour of sanctity; no others of the faithful were interred in the same place: they feared to confound the remains of the one with the remains of the other; hence arose the custom of distinguishing the bodies of martyrs by some symbol, which designated the kind of death they had suffered.

It was a part of the religion of the Jews to raise synagogues and oratories near to the tombs of those who had lived a good life, and to congregate there together to pray. The Greeks offered sacrifices near the places which were set apart for sepulchres, and it is an opinion, tolerably well founded, that the temples of fabulous divinities were raised over the tombs of the heroes of antiquity. It was customary among the Romans to construct over their Apogœa, halls in which they assembled to pay their last

(¹) St. Jerome states that he visited the catacombs every Sunday. "When I found myself," says he, "in that profound obscurity, I thought the expression of the Psalmist verified.—Descendit in infernum vivens."—(*Hieron. in Ezech. c.* 4, *Greg. Turon. l.* 1, *H. Fr. c.* 39.)

duties to the dead, and to perform those ceremonies which were usual in similar cases. They had also chapels and altars, on which they sacrificed to the god *Manes*. Following these examples, the early Christians undoubtedly built over the catacombs those retreats which the lovers of antiquity regard with so much veneration. They repaired thither in crowds, and performed the mysteries of their religion, and of the Agapes, used at funerals. They also raised altars over the tombs of martyrs; they purified the ceremonies of the Pagans; and they gratified a feeling with which piety and devotion had inspired them.

This enthusiasm did not prevent the Christians from seeking to prevent those evils which might result from collecting together all these bodies in places where they assembled; they were careful to fill with earth the spaces which were found empty in different parts of the catacombs.—(*Vide Boldetti Arringo, Marangoni, &c.*)

However, the number of believers increased daily, and the fire of persecution was not less ardent. It seemed as though a moment's truce was only given in order to recommence this species of warfare with the greater fury; the number of martyrs was surprising, and the burial places originally employed were now no longer sufficient.

Some influential citizens having embraced the Christian religion, applied their riches and the lands which they possessed to supply the deficiency. Many patricians, and some pious Roman ladies gave also vast portions of land, to be appropriated to this purpose. Such was the origin of cemeteries. (¹) In these same places altars were raised and chapels constructed, which served as retreats during funeral ceremonies, and during other assemblings for religious purposes.

Ambition, restless and extravagant, had almost thrown the law of the Twelve Tables into oblivion, when the Emperor Adrian restored it to its ancient power. Antoninus Pius extended it to the entire empire; a new law, or one which is just renewed, is always strictly observed. Their dead were then carried out of the city; but they soon again relapsed, and one hundred and fifty years afterwards, Diocletian and Maximian were obliged to enforce it by new decrees.

In the three first ages of the Church, the difficult circumstances in which Christians were placed, their situation in relation to the government and legislation of the Cæsars, served to maintain the custom, which they had practised from the very commencement of Christianity.

(¹) In the environs of ancient Rome there were more than forty cemeteries. Ecclesiastical History has preserved the names of them.—(*Vide Baron ad. an. 226. Panv. Hospin.*) And *Prud.* gives a beautiful description of them, Hymn 11.

Cemeteries were so called from the word *dormire*, a place in which to sleep. We have always been struck with the resemblance between sleep and death. Pausanias relates, that on the tomb of Cypselus there is an engraving of a female representing Night, holding two infants in her arms; in the right, a white infant reposing; it was sleep: in the left, a black infant, also reposing; it was death.—(*Sp. p.* 66.)

At length the Church saw a calm and serene day dawning over its horizon. Constantine, by embracing the Christian religion, established peace. The temples of idols had already for some time been out of favour; in them assemblies were no longer held; but, after having been purified, these edifices became the sanctuary of the true God. The same altars on which the holy mysteries had been celebrated, in the obscurity of the catacombs and cemeteries, were now removed into the cities. (¹) For the first time the tombs of the martyrs occupied the place of the profane divinities. It was this revolution which substituted the heroes of the Christian religion for the heroes of the age. In the churches there was but one sacrifice and one altar, and the unity of the religion would have been thought deficient if the faithful had been exposed to a divided worship. (²)

They then ornamented the cemeteries with much care; and all, in progress of time, became temples,

(¹) In the second century the Christians had churches: their situation, but not their construction, was known. The church of Antioch, which the Emperor Diocletian destroyed, was built in the third century. The altars then were not always raised upon the relics of martyrs. It was not till peace was restored to the Church that tombs were transferred to the cities.

(*) (*Ign. ad. Philadelph. Euseb. H. F. l.* 10, *c.* 4). This was the origin of basilicks, and the principal churches, upon which the others depended and formed part. All Christians of one district recognized one altar and one sacrifice, offered by the same Bishop. There were oratories in the suburbs, which depended upon some principal church.

specially consecrated. (¹)   A short time afterwards, Pope Julius was obliged to construct three ceme- teries along the same roads in which the tombs of Roman families had formerly been placed ; then others were constructed, and the date of their estab- lishment was indicated by their inscriptions.   The desire of having tombs in the interior of towns seemed to increase by impediments.   The fervour of primitive Christianity was displayed in all its vigour : to be interred near those whose memory was held in veneration, was regarded as an enviable privilege ; all wished to be sure of occupying, after death, the very places in which those holy persons had addressed their prayers to God.   Lastly, they extended their confidence so far as to believe that emanations from the bodies of saints were capable of warming the hearts of the faithful, and conveying to them those happy impressions which dispose to fer- vour and to piety.

THE PERIOD IN WHICH THE FIRST CHANGES OCCURRED RESPECTING INTERMENTS IN TOWNS AND CHURCHES.

Fresh additions increased the number of tombs in the catacombs.   Hitherto there had been no distinction for Priests, Bishops, Princes, nor even

(¹) The places in which tombs had been erected often became the sites of temples, even among the Pagans ; on which account, the words *temple* and *sepulchre* are often employed synonymously ; thus Virgil says ;—

Præterea fuit in tectis de marmore templum,
Conjugis antiqui miro quod honore colebat.

for the Popes, if their piety, liberality, and zeal for religion, had not rendered them worthy of this honour. When the Church, from a motive of gratitude, conferred on Constantine the privilege of being buried in the vestibule of the temple of the holy Apostles, which he himself had built, this concession was regarded as a very remarkable testimony of honour and distinction. St. Chrysostome, to impress upon the faithful the full extent and importance of such a privilege, states (1) that the greatest Prince of the earth regarded it as a new lustre to his supreme dignity.

Other successors of Constantine obtained afterwards the same honour; and it was for a long time reserved for those Princes who boldly declared themselves the protectors of the Church. Sometimes it was granted to benefactors who had provided liberally for the decorations of altars, and for the expenses necessarily incurred in performing the august ceremonies of religion. The resemblance between imperial power and the priesthood procured afterwards the same privilege for the Bishops. Their sanctity, and the eminence of their situation, justified this innovation in the discipline of the Church. The motives which rendered this distinc-

(1) *Constantinum Magnum filius ingenti honore se adfecturum existimavit, si eum in Piscatoris vestibulo conderet; quodque imperatoribus sunt in aulis janitores, hoc in sepulchro Piscatoribus sunt imperatores. Atque illi quidem veluti domini interiores loci partes obtinent; hi autem veluti accolæ, et vicini præclarè secum agi putant; si ipsis vestibuli janua adsignetur.* —(Hom. 26 in II. Epist. Cor.)

tion valuable, so deeply concerned the interests of piety and religion, that it was not sought after by the majority of believers. The priesthood, the cloister, and irreprochable morals, were titles necessary to obtain it. The laity, to whom no elevation of rank could confer a claim, endeavoured to obtain the privilege by presenting handsome donations to the church, and distributing alms with liberality. ([1])

So rapid a revolution was not general; many Churches shewed great attachment to ancient rules, and were more rigid as to the exceptions. This change could only be the effect of a relaxation in dis cipline relative to an object to which both Popes and Bishops could present more or less of opposition ; for which reason, ecclesiastical history, during this period, furnishes statements which appear contradictory. In some Churches, at certain epochs, the exception had not as yet been admitted, ([2]) whilst in many others it had been granted to all Ecclesiastics. The more

([1]) Thomassin assigns this as the period of the relaxation of discipline relative to sepulchres.—(*Part* 3, *l.* 1, *c.* 65, § 2, *and also Greg.*)

([2]) This exception commenced in favour of persons of exemplary piety. Muratori has demonstrated that this custom was not introduced at the time of the Pontificate of St. Gregory, by the superstition or cupidity of the Ecclesiastics, as Kepper pretends. The most ancient examples he adduces, which do not go further back than the fourth or fifth century, are all of persons distinguished for their piety. A holy humility frequently determined Bishops not to make use of this prerogative, thinking themselves unworthy of it.—(*Vide* MURATORI *Anecd. t.* 1, *disq.* 17, *et t.* 2, *disq.* 3)

respectable seculars soon received this honour.
The arrangements having been left entirely to the
Bishops, it is not difficult to understand how, in one
Church, eminent dignity or singular piety were the
only grounds for anticipating this distinction, whilst
in another it was very easily obtained; so far,
indeed, was the abuse afterwards carried, that
interment in churches was granted to Pagans and
Christians, to the impious and the holy. Notwithstanding these variations, they did not change the
place in which they had at first resolved to erect
the public tombs, and those to whom the honour of
sepulchre in the city was granted, were always
small in number.

INTRODUCTION OF BURIAL PLACES INTO TOWNS AND CHURCHES.

Up to this time they had not dared to penetrate
into the interior of churches; they had not yet
determined to mix the bodies of the profane (¹)

(¹) This is proved by the following passages :—*Singulare hoc
erat quorundam sanctitatis privilegium alias enim ecclesias
mortuorum cadaveribus pollui non patiebantur.*—(MARTEN *de
Antiq. Monac. rit. l.* 5, *c.* 10, § 97, *seq.* 2.) The Deacon, S.
Ephren, also proves it in a striking passage : *Si quis,* inquit
*fallacibus rationibus ausus fuerit sub altari me conlocari, su-
pernum ac cœleste altare talis nunquam videat ; non enim decet
vermem putredine scatentem in templo et sanctuario me poni ;
sed neque in alio loco templi permittatis reponi.*—(*Test. c.* 2,
Vid. MARTEN *loc. cit.*) Van Epsen assures us that the Christian Emperors always censured the custom of burial in cities ;

with those of martyrs and saints, and thus to break the unity of altars and sacrifices. The tombs were placed along the walls, near to, and without the churches. As people met there to perform the duties of religion, it was soon necessary to protect the faithful from exposure to the weather.([1]) With this view they constructed vestibules and porticoes, and this is the reason also why cemeteries were always near to parish churches. We have yet some remains of this point of antiquity. In some vestibules or porticoes there were small subterraneous chambers and arcades, which were made without and along the walls of the temples—they were called *Exedræ*, and were found in some churches in the time of Baluse. ([2])

they feared contagion : *Imperatores Christiani sanctitatem civitatum violari credebant per corpora mortuorum, quod nimio suo fœtore civitates infecerunt.*—(*T.* 2, sect. 4, tit. 7, c. 2.)

Non defunctorum causâ, sed vivorum inventa est sepultura, ut corpora et visu et odore fœdo amoverentur.—(SENEC. *Excerp. Op. t.* 2.)

([1]) Such was the origin of chapels. The faithful repaired thither when they wished to retire, to meditate or to pray over the tombs. At first these small buildings were separated from the church ; afterwards they were joined to it by means of porticoes and arcades, which are particularly used in the construction of basilicks ; finally they were covered in, and formed, with the rest, the body of the building. The tombs in them became altars, and under the Pontificate of Gregory the Great, the number of them was considerably increased.—(THOMASSIN, *l.* 3, *c.* 66, 5.)

([2]) It was customary to build chapels and oratories in the vicinity of cemeteries ; many of these grounds were at first out of the walls of the cities, and when these were enlarged, the cemeteries were found within their boundaries.

It appears unquestionable that the number of inhumations had greatly increased in Constantinople and in the other towns of the empire, since in accordance with the Emperors Gratian and Valentine the Second, Theodosius the Great, a Prince of exemplary piety, whose zeal for the well-being of the Church is generally acknowledged, was obliged to renew the edicts of his predecessor, and to publish the famous constitution called the *Theodosian Code*. (¹) His design was to prevent the infection of the atmosphere, which so many funerals would necessarily occasion. He forbade the interment of the dead in the interior of cities, and what is still stronger, he ordered that the bodies, the

(') This law is dated A.D. 381. It is found in *Code Theodos. l.* 9, *tit.* 17, *c.* 6. These are the words,—*Omnia quæ supra terram urnis clausa vel sarcofagis corpora detinentur extra urbem delata ponantur, ut et humanitatis instar exhibeant, et relinquant incolarum domicilio sanctitatem.* It not only requires that tombs should be placed out of the city, but speaks in particular of the church of the Holy Apostles at Constantinople, and of the small edifices that had since been raised in cities to the honour of holy martyrs. This wise Emperor was not willing that this example should be made use of as a pretext to vanity and ambition to elude the law. To prove this it will be sufficient to read the terms of the law itself:—*Ac ne alicujus fallax et arguta solertia ab hujus se præcepti intentione subducat, atque apostolorum vel martyrum sedem humandis corporibus existimet esse concessam, ab his quoque ita ut a reliquo civitatis noverint se atque intelligant esse submotos.* From this the Emperor Justinian derived the law which he inserted in his new code. (This is the tenth law, cod. de sacros Eccl.) *Nemo apostolorum et martyrum sedem humanis* (humandis) *corporibus existimet esse concessam.*

urns, and the monuments which were in the city of Rome, should be carried without the walls. The Emperor desired that on this point, modern Rome should equal ancient Rome. This decree was soon carried into effect throughout the whole Roman empire.

If we run through ecclesiastical history, we shall see that the custom of interring in churches was already very prevalent. In one place it had been introduced from pious motives; in another, the space in the neighbouring cemeteries was found too small; similar exceptions were always justified upon the plea of merit or necessity; but they were not allowed until after the most rigid examination. (¹)

St. Ambrose buried his brother Satyrus in the temple of Milan, near the martyr, St. Victor. He, himself, wished to be interred near the remains of St. Jervis and St. Prolais, which he had placed under the altar; and Marcellina, his sister, desired to be carried from Rome to Milan, to be buried with her brothers. " *St. Paulin,*" Bishop of Nola, at the entreaty of a lady of distinction, placed the bodies of her two sons, Cenegius and Celsus, near the tomb of the martyrs. St. Cesaire, Bishop of

(¹) Bede *H. l.* 2, *c.* 3 furnishes an example which proves that burials were not made in churches except in cases of necessity. St. Austin, the Apostle of England, was buried under the portico of the cathedral of which he was Bishop. All those who succeeded him, in the See of Canterbury, were placed under the same portico, until at last, wanting room for tombs, it was determined to place them in the interior of the church.

Arles, was interred in the church which he had built, and where, moreover, he had placed tombs for virgins who had consecrated themselves to God, and for Cesaria, his sister. We read that during the same period, many persons were buried outside the churches. St. Fulgence, a Bishop, was the first of his church who obtained the honour of sepulchre in it. He was a disciple of St. Augustin, and died some time after him. In this church, more than in any other, they conformed to the holy canons and to the laws of the Emperors.—We may also presume that the infraction of these laws had been very rare, and if the expressions of ancient historians lead us to suppose that many persons were interred near the martyrs, we ought to give a different interpretation to them, and suppose that these inhumations were made in the neighbourhood of the churches where the remains of these holy personages reposed. The Monks, whose rules had been made in times of fervour, and who strictly observed the rules, conducted themselves on this point with the most austere severity. Those who inhabited grottoes and deserts were buried in forests and in the hearts of mountains.

Religious orders, associated to monasteries under well known rules, were, for a long time, attached to the ancient discipline of the Church. They employed common cemeteries, placed without the walls of the monasteries, and carried their dead there in carriages. St. Benedict, himself, received no kind of distinction in this particular ; it was not

E

until a much later period that they, for the first time, thought of interring any one in the interior of monasteries.

Walfred, Abbot of Palazzolo, in Tuscany, was the first who, in the eighth century, wished to be buried in his own cloister. Sepulchres were soon afterwards introduced into churches; at length they were introduced into the choir, or what seems more probable, into the chapter. We do not, however, find any vestiges of such an innovation before the ninth century.

Customs so opposite, and which suppose contrary principles, arose from the dispute, which had been vehemently discussed among Christians, long before the time of St. Augustine, viz. how far it was advantageous for interments to be made in places destined for the sepulchre of holy martyrs. St. Augustine was consulted on this subject by *Paulinus*, which induced him to compose his work " On the Duties we owe to the Dead." He there declares a doctrine greatly opposed to that which sprung up in the middle and darker ages. This question was renewed in the time of Gregory the Great. It was also much agitated in the pontificate of Nicholas the First, who was consulted on this subject by the Bulgarians. The answers of this Pontiff led to no other conclusion than that the whole advantage depended upon the good conduct of the deceased, and the fervent prayers of the faithful.

Notwithstanding this diversity of customs, it is

certain that the prohibition of the Emperor Theodosius continued to be respected; it brought back this point of discipline to its original condition. The dead, in general, were removed to a distance from churches, and the honour of being buried without, near to the walls, was considered a very distinguished privilege.

The ordinance of the Emperor Theodosius was probably longer observed, either because the memory of so great a Prince was held in the highest respect, or because his descendants exerted themselves strenuously to maintain this ordinance in its full and entire extent. According to the writings of Gregory the Great, it seems that, from his time, abuses began to spread. Considerable offerings from the rich, procured admission to an honour which ought to have been granted to merit alone, or to superior station. But long before Gregory the Great, the prohibition of Theodosius had been neglected, since this Prince renewed it in Italy, by the advice of the pious and learned Cassiodorus. In fact, it was in Italy that the infraction of the civil and ecclesiastical ordinances concerning burials was the most common.

These observations lead to an important reflection. Whatever difference there may have been in the mode of thinking between Pagans and Christians on the subject of a future state—whatever changes may have been effected in the ceremonies and customs of the Christian Church, we always see that the most enlightened Princes have maintained, by the laws of their government, in regard to sepulchres, that which was most conducive to the good of the people. The ancient Ecclesiastical Constitution—the bulls of the Popes—that inviolable tradition which they endeavoured to establish,—all concurred to preserve cities from the infection of the dead : but this abuse, far from being destroyed, acquired new strength. The many reasons advanced to remove the dread entertained of the dangers of putrefaction,—the flattering hopes they indulged of participating in the merits of the just, by mixing with their tombs,—the distinctions of those who had been judged worthy of this honour, warmed the religious zeal of some, and excited the self love of others. At length the prevailing custom was directly opposed to the established law—the prerogative, which originally was reserved for Emperors, became the portion of the lowest class of citizens, and that which at first was a distinction, became a right, common to every one.

AUTHORITIES OF COUNCILS AGAINST THE ABUSES AND DANGERS OF SEPULCHRE.

From the sixth age, in which, as we have seen, abuses relative to sepulchres were very prevalent in cities ; not only synods, but even councils endeavoured to abolish them, and to restore the ancient discipline of the Church. The Council of Bracar, ([1])

([1]) An. Christi, 563, Concil Bracar can. 18, ib. *Firmissimum usque nunc retinent hoc privilegium civitates Galliæ, et nullo*

held at Brague, published a celebrated canon, by which, not only interment in churches was prohibited, but cities even had the right of preventing any individual from being buried within the precincts of their walls.

We may here again advert to the privilege which martyrs enjoyed in the early ages of Christianity, viz. that of excluding all bodies from the place where they themselves were buried.

The Council of Auxerre ([1]) endeavoured to prevent inhumation in the interior of *baptisteries* either because by this name was understood those edifices which were built in the neighbourhood of temples, to administer there the sacrament of baptism, or because they wished to designate the churches themselves, in the vestibules of which they began in this age to build baptismal fonts. Gregory the Great often so expresses himself in his works, as to lead to the belief that he did not think on this point like the vulgar. He often mentions, with grief, that voluntary offerings made to churches had then become the only means of obtaining sepulchre there. ([2])

modo intra ambitum murorum civitatum cujuslibet defuncti corpus sit humatum Placuit corpora defunctorum nullo modo intra basilicam S. sepeliantur; sed si necesse est, deforis circa murum basilicæ usque a Deo non abhorret.

([1]) An. Christi, 585, c. 15, ib. *Non licet in baptisterio corpora sepelire.* At the same council it was forbidden to place one corpse upon another, that is to say, upon one not entirely consumed.— *(Fleur ad h. A.)*

([2]) L. 7. ep. 4, conf. Thomassin, l. c. These are the very words

54

An age passed away.—The barriers which had been opposed to this custom became too weak ;—it had taken deep root in the West, and was there almost general, while it was scarcely known in the East.

A new epoch, happily for the Church, through another circumstance, fixed the attention of Bishops upon this subject. Charlemagne, at the end of the eighth century, and the commencement of the ninth, occupied himself in restoring the arts and sciences, and the discipline of the Church. He assembled frequent councils in different parts of his kingdom, and the results of these councils gave rise to those public statutes which are so often spoken of in history.

Theodolphus, an Italian by birth, Bishop of Orleans, eminently distinguished in that period, and highly esteemed by Charlemagne, complained that the churches of France had almost become cemeteries. (¹)

of the holy Pontiff Gregory, ep. 56:—*Siquando aliquem in ecclesiâ vestrâ sepeliri conceditis, siquidem parentes ipsius, proximi, vel hœredes pro luminaribus sponte quid offerre voluerint, accipere non vetamus ; peti vero, aut aliquid exigi omnino prohibemus, ne, quod valdè irreligiosum est, aut venalis fortasse, quod absit ducatur Ecclesia, aut vos de humanis videamini mortibus gratulari, si ex eorum cadaveribus studeatis quærere quolibet modo compendium.*

(¹) An. Ch. 794. In his reign care was taken that all the canons should be scrupulously observed, particularly those which related to sepulchres.—(Theodolph. cap. ad par. c. 9.) These are his own words :—*Loca divino cultui mancipata et ad offerendas hostias præparata, cæmeteria, sive polyandria facta sunt ; undè*

He therefore demanded that no priest or layman should be interred in the church, unless he had recommended himself by the sanctity of his life. As to the tombs, he had them destroyed, and ordered that, for the future, they should not be raised above the earth. He added, moreover, that if they could not execute this precept, they should remove the altar, carry it to another place, and make only a cemetery of the church. [1]

The statutes of Charlemagne, before mentioned, in order to put an end to the quarrels which had arisen between Theodolphus and the other prelates of France, deprived the laity of sepulchre in the interior of churches, and, ultimately, altogether pro-

volumus ut ab hac re deinceps abstineatur, et nemo in ecclesiâ sepeliatur, nisi forte talis sit persona sacerdotis aut cujuslibet justi hominis, quæ per vitæ meritum talem vivendo suo corpori defuncto locum adquisivit. If this law had been exactly followed, there would have been but little occasion for apprehension ; but self love soon endeavoured to usurp what was only really due to a small number of virtuous persons, which always happens when opinion alone decides upon prerogatives.

Corpora vero, continues Theodolphus, *quæ antiquitùs in ecclesiis sepulta sunt nequaquam projiciantur, sed tumuli qui adparent profundius in terram mittantur ; et pavimento desuper facto, nullo tumulorum vestigio ad parente ecclesiæ reverentia conservetur. Ubi vero est tanta cadaverum multitudo, ut hoc facere difficile sit, locus ille pro cæmeterio habeatur, ablato inde altari, et in eo loco constructo ubi religiosè et purè Deo sacrificium offerri valeat.*

[1] According to St. Chrysostome, cemeteries were to be placed beyond the gates of cities.

hibited it. (¹) The Sixth Council of Arles, (²) and the Council of Magouza (³) permitted only Bishops, Abbots, and Ecclesiastics, or laymen of the first distinction, to be interred in churches. Hincmar, Archbishop of Rheims, without controversy the greatest man of his age, extracted from the works of St. Gregory some very important information upon this point. Wishing entirely to eradicate this abuse, he obliged the Bishops of his diocese to make oath that from that time they would require no remuneration for interments. (⁴) The Council of Meaux (⁵) enforced the same regulations. Hincmar further positively ordered that they should be very circumspect in regard to interments within the churches. (⁶) The donations of Christians were at first voluntary ; custom soon rendered them compulsory. Erasdus, Archbishop of Tours, forbade in his diocese anything being demanded in any place whatever, where burial was performed. The Council of Nantes allowed tombs to be raised in the vestibules

(¹) An. 797, l. 1, c. 559, and l. 5, c. 48.

Nullus deinceps in ecclesia mortuum sepeliat.

(²) An. 813, can. 21. *De sepeliendis in basilicis mortuis constitutio illa servetur quæ antiquis patribus constituta est.*

(³) An. evd. conc. Mag. c. 20.

(⁴) An. 845.

(⁵) Couc. Meld. an. eod. c. 72.

(⁶) Hincmar prohibited and abolished hereditary tombs, and empowered his curates to make such regulations upon this subject as they judged proper. *Nemo Christianorum præsumant quasi haereditario jure de sepulturâ contendere, sed in sacerdotis providentiâ sit.*

and porticoes, but formally interdicted their construction in churches. ([1])

The Council of Tribur ([2]) exhorted the nobles to be contented with having their sepulchres near the cathedral, or, if they wished it, near the convents and monasteries. Moreover, the Bishops and curates were the only dispensers of this favour among the Gauls. It appears from the reply of Nicholas I. to the Bulgarians, ([3]) that in Italy a person was admitted to participate in this honour who was not absolutely an abandoned character; whilst in Gaul it was necessary to be distinguished by singular piety.

Customs on this point were not the less various in the Levant. According to the verses attributed to St. Gregory, of Naziance, it seems that from the fourth age the custom of interment in churches was adopted. He himself attests it in the case of his brother Cæsarius; ([4]) and St. Gregory, of Nice, tells us, that his sister

([1]) This happened at the end of the ninth century, although some place it more than two centuries earlier. The words of this Council deserve to be faithfully recorded. *Prohibendum est etiam secundum majorum instituta, ut in ecclesiâ nullatenus sepeliantur, sed in atrio aut in porticis, aut in exedris ecclesiae. Intra ecclesiam vero et propè altare ubi corpus Domini et sanguis conficiuntur nullatenus sepeliantur.*—Labbe t. 9 conc.—All Councils agree in ordering the tradition of the ancients to be followed; that is to say, to observe scrupulously this prohibition.

([2]) An. Ch. 895, c. 15.

([3]) 865. A little before the two Councils above cited.

([4]) Orat. 10.

Macrina was interred near the holy martyrs, in the same church where their mother had formerly been buried. (¹) We see, however, in this interval, that the Emperors and other grandees of the kingdom had been buried without the temple. The tombs of Theodsius himself, of Arcadius and Honorius, his sons,—Theodsius the younger,—of Eudocia and of Jovier, were placed in the portico of the basilick of the holy Apostles, at Constantinople. (²)

They were obliged from time to time to enforce this custom, as is clearly seen in the letters of Balsamon to Marcus, patriarch of Alexandria, to whom he says, (³) that according to the ancient statutes, no one should be interred in churches consecrated by the Bishops, and where the relics of the saints reposed. Thus the law ordained, as expressed in the following terms:—" Nullus in ecclesia mortuus sepeliatur ;" (⁴) and the well known canon expressly says, " Non licet quemquam sepelire in ecclesia, ubi scilicet corpus martyris depositum est. (⁵)

The Emperor Leo, surnamed the Philosoper, who finished the great work begun by his father, Basil of Macedonia, that is to say, the collection and publication of the basilicks (canons of the church),

(¹) In. Vit. B. Macrin.
(²) Niceph. l. 14, c. 58.
(³) Resp. ad. interr. 38.
(⁴) Basilic. l. 5, t. 1, c. 2, l. 6. Code Theod. *de Sep. Viol.*
(⁵) If, in the facts we relate concerning sepulchres, there are some which appear opposite and contradictory, this only proves that there were laws and exceptions to those laws ; but the spirit of the Church has never varied on this subject.

erased in one of his statutes the old prohibition of burying in churches. The terms of his decree leave no doubt as to the discredit and disuse into which this prohibition had fallen. He chose rather to dispense with a law which was no longer observed, than to compromise his authority by uselessly endeavouring to enforce it, however advantageous it might be. ([1])

Fortunately, the new law of the Emperor Leo had no force in the West, and soon ceased to be observed in the East. We must admit, however, that discipline was afterwards much relaxed. It is equally certain, that the Church, always animated by the same spirit, never ceased as much as possible to re-establish ancient customs. The councils held, from the 10th to the 18th century, in many parts of the Catholic world, are incontestable evidences of this. We have a Council of Ravenna, under Gilbert, and afterwards under Sylvester II, in 995; the sixth of Winchester, 1076; the famous Synod of Toulouse in 1093, in which it was determined to make two cemeteries, one for the Bishops and nobles, the other for the common inhabitants; a Council at London in 1107; one at Cognac 1255 and 1260;

([1]) An. Ch. 886, nov. 53. *Ne igitur ullo modo inter similes leges hæc lex censeatur sancimus; quin potius ut a Consuetridine certe contemnitur, sic etiam decreto nostro prorsus reprobatur.* At the same time he gives two reasons for the non-observance. The first was, the grief at seeing the bodies of relatives so far removed; the second, the expense of transportation, which was necessarily burthensome to the poor.

one at Bude in 1269; one at Nismes in 1284; one at Chester in 1292; one at Avignon in 1326; one at Narbonne in 1551; one at Toledo in 1556; one at Malines in 1570; a Committee of the Clergy of France, assembled at Melun in 1579; a Synod at Rouen in 1581; at Rheims in 1583; one at Bordeaux and at Tours in the same year; one at Bruges in 1584; one at Aix in 1585; one at Toulouse in 1590; another at Narbonne and one at Bordeaux in 1624: all these have given on this subject the same precepts, and admitted the same doctrine. (¹)

In the course of so many ages which had passed away from the pontificate of Gregory to the Council of Trent, they always endeavoured to shelter the Church from the suspicion of seeking to derive the slightest remuneration from interment in churches. Exactions were proscribed, but voluntary offerings were always made, and they were not refused. The difficulty of prevailing on churches to give up this source of revenue, had always presented

(¹) It would be tedious to state entire the canons of these councils: some regard directly the subject here treated; others indirectly. Some forbid sepulchres to be sold. A canon of the Synod of Rouen prohibits interment in churches; it allows an exception only in favour of eminent Ecclesiastics, of persons in high station, of men of eminent virtue. *Cæteri religiose in Cœmeteriis tradantur.* A canon of the Council of Bordeaux admits sepulchre in the interior of churches only to Bishops, curates, regulars, patrons; it excludes all others if they have not the especial consent of the Bishop. The canon of Tours runs thus:—*Laicis omnibus, etiam nobilibus, minimè liceat sepulturas in ecclesiis jure proprio sibi vindicare, quum sepultura sit propriè et merè jus spiritale et ecclesiasticum*

powerful obstacles in the way of those Bishops who were zealous for the ancient discipline. Ambition afforded fresh obstacles to St. Charles Boromée, Archbishop of Milan, which hindered him from remedying at once those abuses of which for a long time he had complained. If, on the one hand, they could have destroyed the spirit of interest in persons attached to the Church, and, on the other hand, if Christians had never seen anything in the difference of burials which could interest their self-love, every thing would have soon changed its appearance, and the ancient use of cemeteries would have been re-established. [1] The holy Bishop of Milan desired it greatly, and we see in his first council the ardent wishes he had entertained that this point of discipline should be entirely established.

In this design he openly opposed the ambition of the great, who maintained this abuse. He was not ignorant that at first graves were chosen in the neighbourhood of churches through piety; that afterwards the desire of distinction penetrated into the interior of temples; and that, at length, this permission having become easy and general, it was no longer possible to become distinguished except by the position of the tombs, and the magnificence of their decoration. The holy canons had foreseen these dangers, and they were at all times opposed to such abuses.

This holy Bishop wished to remove from burial

[1] An. Ch. 1565. *Morem restituendum curent (episcopi) in cemeteriis sepeliendi*, c. 61.

places escutcheons, portraits, images, and all those ornaments invented by vanity, and which ill-accorded with the sad and miserable condition of the dead. He himself set the example in his own cathedral. A magnificent tomb, raised to the memory of one of his ancestors, by order of Pope Pius IV. Bishop of Rome, was not spared. He excepted that which related to the glory of Kings, and to the majesty of the throne. In his fourth council, this holy Pontiff also engaged his Bishops [1] anew to observe the valuable laws and usages of the earlier times. This reform was adopted somewhat generally, and Pope Pius V. in one of his decrees, forbade all useless pomp [2] in the burial of Christians. He only allowed tombs of marble to be erected, always providing that they should not contain the bodies of those in whose honour they were raised. [3]

May we not conclude from all these authorities, that the custom of interring bodies in churches ought to be proscribed, as contrary to the spirit of our religion. We shall prove in another place that it is not less repugnant to the principles of sound philosophy.

[1] The Romans called an empty tomb, raised in honour of an illustrious dead person, who had from some circumstance been deprived of burial, *cenotaphium.* Then, after having performed the usual ceremonies, they called the dead three times. Thus Æneas says in Virgil.—

Tunc egomet tumulum Rhœteo in littore inanem
Constitui et magnâ manes ter voce vocavi.

[2] 1576.

[3] Const. incip. cum primum apostolatus, § 8.

ORDINANCE OF THE ARCHBISHOP OF TOULOUSE CONCERNING INTERMENT IN CHURCHES.

[This very interesting document is taken from the work of Dr. Pascalis, entitled " An Exposition of the Dangers of Interment in Cities, &c." New York, 1823.]

" *Stephen Charles de Lomenie de Brienne*, by the grace of God and the Holy Apostolic See, Archbishop of Toulouse, Councellor of the King, &c. to all Ecclesiastics, secular or regular, and to all the laity of this diocese, sends greeting and blessing.

" Whereas, the venerable Provost and Clergy of our metropolitan church have represented to us that, in violation of the holy canons, interments in that church have increased exceedingly, and that the air is sensibly contaminated by fetid exhalations from vaults, which are not deep, and are continually re-opened for the admission of fresh bodies.

" Similar complaints have been transmitted to us from several parts of this diocese; and although we have deferred any notice till now, yet our dearly beloved brethren need not accuse us of neglect, delay, or indifference in this important affair. Wise ordinances require much time for consideration, and should be offered to minds prepared to receive them. Measures too prompt might have proved revolting to your sensibilities, or you might have thought such restrictions of your privileges sufficient, as had already been enforced by vanity, or to which custom lent a justification. To secure your docility and compliance, it was necessary that your eyes should be opened to your danger by repeated accidents, sudden deaths, and frequent epidemics. It was necessary that your own wishes, impelled by sad experience, should compel our interference; and that the excess of the evil should call, in a manner, for an excess of precautionary measures.

" Believe not, dearly beloved brethren, that our solicitude and anxious care for the public health is the only motive that induces us to break silence. Such is the harmony always existing between religion and sound policy, that what is acknowledged as decorous and useful by the one, is also commanded and prescribed by the other. To the instinct of self-preservation, which calls loudly for a reformation of the present system of burial, we may add the commands of God, which direct us to be careful of our lives, that we may serve him and prepare for a happy eternity; and the orders of the Church, which have always reprobated as a profanation the general admission of the dead within consecrated walls and in places held sacred; and the dictates of our Christian duties, which require an assiduous attendance at the temple, all pretexts and pretences to the contrary notwithstanding. May our subsequent details and remarks enlighten your piety without enfeebling it; and without impairing the respect due to the memory of the dead, *confound that inconsistent vanity which follows them even into the grave.* (¹)

(¹) *Hæc porro dico, non ut sepulturam tollam, absit ; sed ut luxum et intempestivam ambitionem succidam.*—(St. CHRYS. Hom. 84, in Joann.)

" This respect is a natural sentiment in every stage of society ; and depraved indeed must those be that do not feel it. No social ties could unite us, if death were able instantly to extinguish affection in the hearts of survivors. He who feels no emotions of grief or pity beside the grave of a fellow being, could have borne no love to that being during life. ' We respect,' says St. Augustine, ' every trifle that reminds us of a beloved object ; the ring or the dress worn by a father are dear to his children.' How then can we other than respect the ashes of those who were dear to us ; or how other than endeavour to prolong the existence of their frail remains ?—*(De Civitate Dei,* cap. 13.)

" Religion renders this natural respect stronger, because it informs us that between the happiness of the just and the punishment of the reprobate, there is a middle state for those ' who die well-disposed, but have not yet satisfied divine justice ; and that it is a holy and useful practice to pray for the dead that their sins may be forgiven them.'— (2 Maccab. xii. 46): a sweet and precious doctrine to the dying sinner, and affording also to the afflicted, who have lost companions, friends, or relatives, the consoling task of contributing to their happiness by prayer.

" It would then be an infraction of every law, as say Saint Augustine and Origenus, *to neglect the burial of the dead, as if they were mere brutes ; or to throw away bodies that have been the abodes*

F

of rational souls, and temples of the Holy Ghost.
But these duties have legitimate limits. While
religion regulates all that can be conducive to the
rest of the departed, and permits the indulgence
of a natural sorrow, it forbids every expression
that proceeds from pride and vanity. ' *Why,*'
says St. Jerome, (*in vitâ Pauli*), ' *does a desire for
appearance exist amid mourning and tears ? why
should the dead be clothed in sumptuous vestments?
Cannot the rich rot away unless in the same gor-
geous apparel that decorated them when alive ?*'—
' *Pompous funeral processions,*' adds St. Augustine,
' *and expensive monuments, may perhaps console
the living, but they cannot be of any use to the
dead.*'—' *Of what use to them are these idle distinctions ?*' exclaims St. Chrysostom. ' Their memory and their worth, and not their perishable
remains, should be honoured. Since then ye wish
to give departed friends rational and Christian-like
testimonies of esteem, love, and regret, *do for
them, and for yourselves, all that can contribute to
the glory of God.* If they were virtuous, be so
also ; if vicious, correct the mischief they have
done, and continue whatever good intentions they
may have assumed. It is by the virtues of their
children that parents are honoured in the grave,
and these are their only worthy and acceptable
obsequies.'

" These principles naturally lead us to ascertain
what place then should be appropriated to the disposal of our departed brethren. The custom of

praying for them probably induced the early Christians to deposit them near each other in the same ground; this was the origin of cemeteries. St. Chrysostom informs us (Hom. 84, in Math.) that cemeteries were not permitted in cities, because the presence or vicinity of the dead would not only contaminate pure air, but incommode the inhabitants by the stench they would occasion. *Nullum in civitate sepulchrum struitur.* If such, says a council (Hom. 74), is the privilege of cities, how evident it is that a church has a right to exclude interments from within her walls. In the council of Brague, burials in churches were forbidden, and the house of God was decreed to be open only to the relics of apostles and martyrs. *Nemo Apostolorum vel Martyrum sedem humanis corporibus æstimet esse concessam* (in the year 563, Can. 18.) The bodies of even Emperors were only admitted to the porticoes or chapels of temples. Constantine himself, to whom the Church was so much indebted, and so grateful, asked no higher favour than to be buried under the portico of the church of the Holy Apostles. (Vid. Eusebius, lib. 4, de vitâ Constanti. St. Chrysost. hom. 26, in Corinth.) Martyrs and confessors only were admitted; because, as St. Ambrosius remarks, it was '*just that those who had been victims to their faith should be deposited near the altar where was offered the sacrament of the sacrifice of their divine Lord and Master.* (Vid. St. Ambr. Epist. de Reliq. ss. Gervasii et Protasii.)

" Such was the primitive discipline in relation to interment; and what is more interesting in this statement, dearly beloved brethren, is, that legitimate exceptions have been used as precedents for its infringement, so true it is, that the slightest compromise of a law leads finally to its destruction or total violation.

" Those who, by an exemplary life, had acquired a reputation for holiness, were allowed to partake of the privilege of martyrs; but this holiness was not as easily substantiated as the heroism of those who sealed their faith with their blood; and as the numbers of the Christians increased, proofs became still more difficult and obscure. Indulgence was then used; appearances soon assumed the place of reality, and equivocal signs of piety obtained prerogatives due only to genuine zeal.

" The clergy, on account of their sacred functions, and the nobility, whom their high rank made more desirous to shun the dishonour or scandal of vice, claimed to be interred within the temple. Founders of churches became invested with the same right, and transient benefactors required the same reward for their donations. The descendants of both claimed as a patrimony, that which had only been granted to individual merit. When the privilege was thus general, a refusal was an exception that threw an odium on the unsuccessful applicant. Where the admission of any one was a favour, none could be excluded who had any pretence to offer. In the early ages, burial in Churches had been expressly forbidden, or even inhumation within cities. But, by the gradual increase of a fatal condescension, the evil has arrived at a height that demands attention. Cemeteries, instead of being beyond our walls, are among our habitations, and spread a fetid odour even into the neighbouring houses. *The very churches have become cemeteries.* (¹) The burial of Christians in an open place, set apart for the purpose, is considered a disgrace ; and neither the interruption of the holy offices, occasioned by the repeated interments, nor the smell of the earth, imbued with putrescence, and so often moved ; nor the indecent state of the pavement of our churches, which is not even as solid as the public street, nor our repugnance to consign to the house of the Lord the impure bodies of men worn out with vice and crimes, can check the vanity of the great, whose empty titles and escutcheons must be hung on our pillars for the sake of their empty distinctions, or of the commonalty, who must ape the great. Death at least should level all men ; but its lessons are lost, and the dearest of interests, self-preservation, must yield to the reigning foible.

" The progress of this evil, dearly beloved brethren, may be determined by the efforts of the Church to overcome it. Sometimes her prohibitions have been express; at other times they have been intended to restrict the favour to a few of the

---

(¹) *Loca divino cultui mancipata ad offerandas hostias, cœmeteria, sive polyandria facta sunt.*—(Theodolph. Auvel. cap. 9.)

faithful. When she has permitted interment in the
purlieus or porticoes of temples, (¹) it was to prevent it in the church itself; when she has admitted
all ecclesiastics, it is because they were presupposed
to be all of holy lives; when founders were favoured, and even benefactors, it was to exclude by such
an exception, all others. She permits exceptions
without a view to their becoming hereditary, and
tolerates unfounded rights to endow her ministers
with greater power for the adoption of measures for
the prevention of the evil effects of her former condescension.

" The Gallican Church has shown much zeal in
endeavouring to recal the ancient discipline upon
this point; interment in churches is prohibited by
almot every council held in this kingdom!(²) almost
all our rituals and synodal statutes forbid it; and
latterly, many Bishops, and particularly those of
this province, have done their best to correct this
abuse. (³)

(¹) De Sinodo Cicestr. Ann. 1292, tit. 5. Conc. Labb. tom.
1, part 2.

Ex. statut. Eccles. trec. 1, ann. 374, thes. anecd. tit. 4, coll.
1125.

Concil. Labb. tom. 3, col. 586.

Concil. Labb. tit. 11, part col. 752.

These are simple references to the motives by which the Church
had been induced at different times to admit some exceptions
against interment.

(²) The statutes called *Capitularies,* established by the con-
currence of civil and ecclesiastical authorities, expressly declare :
Nullus deinceps in ecclesiâ mortuus sepeliatur.

(³) The following French Bishops and Archbishops have, at the

" But without derogating from the respect due to their wisdom and their labours, may we not say that this temporizing plan has rendered their whole work useless ?

" If inhumation around churches is to be allowed, can cities be perfectly salubrious ? If priests and laymen, distinguished for piety, are to be buried within, who shall judge of this piety, or who presume to refuse their testimony ? If the quality of founder or of benefactor is a title, what rate shall fix the privilege ? If the right is hereditary, must not time multiply the evil to excess, and will not our churches at length be crowded as now, beyond endurance ? If distinctions in ranks are to exist after death, can vanity know any limitation, or judge ? if these distinctions are to be procured for money, will not vanity lavish riches to procure them ? and would it be proper for the Church to prostitute to wealth, an honour only due to *such as have been rendered worthy by the grace of God?*

affixed dates, promulgated in their sees ordinances against interment in towns or in churches :—De Pericard, Bishop of Avranches, A.D. 1600; Le Commandeur, Bishop of St. Malo, A.D. 1620; De Matignon, Bishop of Lizieux, A.D. 1650 ; De la Guibourgere, first Bishop of La Rochelle, A.D. 1655; Vialart, Bishop of Chalons, A.D. 1661 ; Faur, Bishop of Amiens, A.D. 1662; D'Elbeur, Bishop of Orleans, A.D. 1664; De Pavillon, Bishop of Aleth, A.D. 1670 ; Seven, Bishop of Cahors, A.D. 1673; De Villaserin, Bishop of Senez, A.D. 1672-73; Cardinal le Camus, Bishop of Grenoble, A.D. 1690; De Clermont, Bishop of Noyou, A.D. 1691; De Sillery, Bishop of Soissons, A.D. 1700; De Beson, Archbishop of Rouen, A.D. 1721; and the same year, the Bishop Evreux, and the Archbishop of Auch.

We are disposed, dearly beloved brethren, to show all possible moderation in this necessary reformation; though charged to be strict in the fulfilment of our pastoral duties, we are allowed a discretionary power, and can consult your habits, your opinions, and even your prejudices, and all that may conciliate your interests with the glory of God; but woe to us, if blinded by weakness, we lose sight of the experience of past ages, and suffer things still to continue, that have till now served, and can only serve, to perpetuate the disorder!

" The only real means of reform is to re-establish the ancient rules and observances, as did Pope Urban IV. when he wished to abolish the indecent custom, which had insensibly crept into the church of St. Peter at Rome, of burying together *the pious and the profane, the saint with the sinner, the just with the unjust;* and to unite to the detriment of Christians and the destruction of the respect due to the Church, what God would eternally separate. And St. Charles Borromæus ordered that *the neglected custom of interring in cemeteries should be resumed entirely.* The same was done in the last century by the Bishop of Senlis, and some few having appealed from the ordinance, it was confirmed by the Parliament of Paris. The civil law could not but agree on this point with our religious canons, because the preservation of the lives of the members of a community is a duty of the first magnitude; and it suffices to enter our churches, to be convinced of the baneful effects of the fetid exhalations in them.

" Some of our dearly beloved brethren may blame the rigour of our ordinance ; but can they make any reasonable complaint ? Churches were not intended for sepulchral monuments ; and so little was such a use of them ever expected, that, according to the remark of a celebrated canonist, there is no prayer in the liturgy relating to such a ceremony, while there are some expressly intended for the benediction of burying grounds. And do you think that titles, *whose abuses would continually cry out against them*, are to prevail over the dignity of our temples and the sanctity of our altars ?

" Would you insist for this privilege on account of the standing, the offices, the rank, you hold in society? We have every reason to believe, that those who have the greatest right to the distinction will be the least eager to obtain it. Exceptions are odious, and multiply pretences and objections. Who will dare to complain, when the law is general; and what law can more justly be general than one that relates to the grave?

" Would you say that we are depriving a holy life of its rewards and prerogatives ? If the voice of the public testified to the sanctity of your career, how joyfully would we receive your bodies into our temples, as those of the martyrs were welcomed by the primitive Church ! But piety, while meriting and obtaining the honours reserved for the saints, is far from assuming them as her right : and while she feels that peculiar benedictions have been passed upon public burying grounds, she acknow-

ledges that *the most magnificent obsequies are of
no use to the sinner.*

" Would you reproach us with depriving you of
a right, bought by the donations of your ancestors?
But do you think that those virtuous men, from
whom you are proud to derive your descent, wished
to leave to their posterity a right to disturb our
holy mysteries, and to spread pestilence among
their fellow-citizens? Then take back their gifts,
if these are to be construed into titles in fee simple.
Our rules for the future must not be violated; and
the Church will satisfy your avarice rather than your
pride.

" We will not suspect our worthy coadjutors in
the clerical function of regretting the privilege so
long granted to their holy habits. We are obliged
daily to sacrifice ourselves for the happiness and
weal of our people, and will therefore think the less
of the renunciation of a gratification that might be
harmful to them. Our most precious advantage is
the power we enjoy of being examples to them in
all that is useful and religious; and great indeed
will be our pleasure, if our example engages others
to allow without murmur or complaint, the re-estab-
lishment of a law equally necessary for the good of
society, and of religion.

" Ye whom the vows of the cloister have united
under the yoke of the Lord! will you object to the
retrenchment of your funds that this ordinance must
produce! No; for you wish not to support existence at the expense of the lives of others. We

will do all for you that just toleration will allow; but you yourselves would blame us, if rather than deprive you of a source of revenue, we were to authorize your chapels to continue or to become, centres of infection and death. Render your temples, worthy of the presence of the Deity; gain the attendance of the faithful by assiduous and fervent prayer! inspire confidence by the decorum of your conduct, and the purity of your manners, and you will find the gratitude of the pious lavish alms upon you to supply the loss you have cheerfully undergone for the public weal.

"And you, right worthy magistrates, who are charged with the care of the laws, be assured that it is with no view to pass the bounds of our powers that we revise our canons. We know that interment is a civil affair. We would direct nothing relating to it without your agreement and participation. Then let the perfect accordance of our measures, blend our united decrees into one authority; and while we speak in the name of God, whose ministers we are, secure obedience to our mandates in the name of the King; for this affair touches not only the credit of the Church, but the interest of the people. We have investigated and examined the request of our venerable Chapter; the petitions from divers parts of our diocese; the *proces verbaux* of the inspection of many parishes, from which it appeared that the abuse of church-interment was carried to its height; and, finally, the reports and opinions of physicians on the pernicious consequences of this custom; and *therefore* we, as far as in our power lies, and in full confidence that the civil authorities will sanction our ordinance, have ordained and enacted, and do ordain and enact, &c."([1])

MODERN STATUTES AGAINST INTERMENT IN CHURCHES AND TOWNS.

It may not be amiss to recapitulate what we have clearly proved in the preceding pages. The prohibition of inhumation in towns was established in the Roman law of the Twelve Tables enacted by the Decemviri; it continued to be incorporated in the laws of all the succeeding forms of government. The prohibition after Constantine was explicitly laid down in the code of Theodosius, A.D. 381; and the admission into Churches of the bodies of even holy personages, was pointedly forbidden. The same was renewed in the Justinian code. At the commencement of the sixth century the Senate of Rome had not yet permitted any cemetery in or near the city of Rome. The *Capitularies* or civil and religious statutes of Charlemagne, forbid interment in churches. Though the discipline of the Church after this, through the interested motives of individuals, became relaxed to an alarming degree,

([1]) The provisions of the ordinance against interment in the city of Toulouse are contained in fifteen articles, confirmed in toto, and were sanctioned the ensuing year by the Parliaments in France and by the King. The eloquent Prelate was shortly afterwards raised by Pope Pius VI. to the dignity of Cardinal.

yet continual efforts were made to restore its pris-
tine integrity by the decrees of more than twenty
councils convened at different periods from the 8th
to the 18th century. The Parliament of Paris, in
1765, took a decisive stand against the abuses of interment. It will not be unnecessary to observe,
that Parliaments in France had a portion of legislative and executive authority in their districts, and
were thirteen in number. A Court of Parliament
was also an intermediary power between the people
and the Sovereign, whose orders remained without
force until registered therein. Parliaments, in fine,
were high courts of civil and criminal judicature,
composed of many Presidents, and about thirty
Privy Counsellors. The following decree *(arrêt)*
of the Parliament of Paris is the more remarkable,
because it was occasioned by an almost universal
complaint from the inhabitants of parishes on the
noisome and sickly influence of churches and
cemeteries. It is asserted in the preamble, that
" daily complaints are made on the infectious effect
of the parish cemeteries, especially when the heats
of summer have increased the exhalations ; then the
air is so corrupted, that the most necessary aliments
will only keep a few hours in the neighbouring
houses : this proceeds either from the soil being so
completely saturated that it cannot retain or absorb
any longer the putrescent dissolution, or from the
too circumscribed extent of the ground for the number of dead annually interred. The same spot is
repeatedly used ; and by the carelessness of those

who inter the dead, the graves are, perhaps, often re-opened too soon." The provisions of the act in nineteen articles, are absolute, and admit of no exceptions.

First. All cemeteries and churchyards in the city of Paris were to be closed, and to remain unoccupied for the space of five years, or longer, if thought necessary by proper officers and physicians.

Second. Eight cemeteries were to be established forthwith, at a distance from the suburbs; each to be of a size proportionate to the number of parishes to which it should belong, and to be fenced with a stone wall eight feet in height; an oratory chapel to be erected in the centre, and a small dwelling for the keeper at the gate; the graves not to be marked by stones; and epitaphs, or inscriptions, to be placed on the walls.

Third. To facilitate the transportation of bodies, there was to be a conveniently situated house of deposit for every cemetery; the walls of it to be four feet high, with iron spikes on them; the building six feet high, surmounted with a dome, open at top: one or two rooms to be connected with each place of deposit, where clergymen, selected in rotation, by the rector of the parish, might have charge of the bodies until removed.

Fourth. Every day, at two o'clock in the morning, from the first April to the first October, and from four A. M. from October first to April first, the bodies were to be carried from the deposit to the cemetery, in a hearse, covered with a pall, and drawn by two horses; and the hearse to be attended by one or more clergymen, and some torch bearers, who were to be grave-diggers. In this decree there were no regulations for proprietors of vaults, dignitaries of the Church or public officers, except that, for the sum of two thousand livres, paid to the parish, a body might be consigned to a family vault in a church, if the coffin were of lead: and that the high Ecclesiastics might have their burial in the same manner.

It was thought that the great and populous capital of France would, by this decree, be sufficiently protected against the dangers of city cemeteries and church vaults. But eleven years after (September, 1774), the same authority was obliged to make another decree against opening vaults for the admission of bodies. On this occasion, the Court, repeating in the preamble, the words of the royal attorney, says, that " as the decrees of the Court relating to burial in churches, contain the motives which led to those decrees, it would be useless to repeat them, while reasons, still more pressing, daily call for a strict attention to the re-opening of vaults, the fatal consequences of which demand a general law, to be put in force against all interment in churches whatever. This abuse, introduced by pride and vanity, is now often laid aside by Christian humility, and the noblest have requested to be interred in cemeteries. This Court will reinstate the ancient discipline of the Church, and give a new sanction to the rescripts of those Sovereigns who maintained it by their authority: the temples will then resume the decency and order of appearance which they cannot display while the opening of vaults is permitted; they will also be freed from the fetid smells which render the air in them insalubrious, and which are, perhaps, the principal cause of the distressing epidemics that have appeared in the provinces. The general complaint against the practice of church vaults is the strongest argument in favour of this decree. The Bishops of such places as were afflicted by it, have issued ordinances, and laid them before this Court for confirmation, which has been granted to some, and solicited by others: pastors of the second degree have united with the higher dignitaries in petitioning for a civil regulation on this point. Medical men assure us, that the vapours exhaling from putrefaction, fill the air with chemical compounds, dangerous to health and productive of malignant diseases. The epidemics which prevail in the warm season confirm their assertion. We know, however, that this decree is against the wishes of a certain class, who found claims upon a possession in itself an abuse, or upon titles yielded through complaisance, or obtained without any legitimate grant, or upon a permission acquired by means of a small sum, which they imagine entails an hereditary right to burial within a church; as if possession were a right superior to justice, or that a prescriptive indulgence should be continued in despite of its injury to the public good ; or that a certain sum of money were an equivalent for the health and life of their fellow citizens. But these objections are of little moment, and must yield to considerations of the public weal ; and, no doubt, those very individuals, if they can cast aside their erroneous prejudices and prepossessions, and look only to the advantage of their fellow citizens, will join with the majority in applauding this decree. The articles 13 and 14 of the ordinance of Francis I. may be cited on this subject ; they run thus :—" *We have ordained, that no one, of whatsoever quality or condition he may be, can pretend to a right, possession, prerogative, &c. in a church or temple, to &c. &c. &c. graves or vaults, &c. unless he be a patron or founder of the said church or temple, with letters of credence to that effect, or sentence legally pronounced in his favour, on these grounds.* It is, moreover, an acceptable service in those intrusted with the power of watching over the welfare of their fellow citizens, to extend their solicitude to the preservation of the public health, by using the most efficacious means for removing the causes of disease. This object alone, independent of any other, would have been sufficient to determine this Court to institute the following requisitions," &c. The decree extends its prohibitions to all the churches within the jurisdictional district of the Court ; and reduces the right of burial to the ministry of those churches ; to patrons, founders, Lord Chief Justices ; and such, in fine, as have titles,

G

in good and due form, justifying their possession, by inheritance, from concessions granted by the Church in favour of great donations, &c.

These Parliamentary acts prepared the way to a universal reformation of the abuses of interment, not only because they gradually weaned the spiritual and temporal Lords, and the rich, from seeking so unstable a privilege as the right of burial in churches, but because they were enacted in accordance with public opinion. Louis XV. concurring entirely in the prohibition of city grave yards, by the Parliament of Paris, granted to the parish of Saint Louis, at Versailles, one hundred and sixty perches of land (three thousand six hundred square feet) in the forest of Satori, to be used as a cemetery, in place of the old one. Louis XVI. took a still more active part, by a royal declaration, dated March, 1776, the preamble of which thus sets forth :—" That the Archbishops, Bishops, and other Ecclesiastics, in Council assembled, last year, in our good city of Paris, have represented to us, that for many years complaints have been made to them from different parts of their respective dioceses, on the frequent inhumations in churches, and also on the actual situation of their cemeteries, which are too near the said churches, and might be placed more advantageously if removed to a distance from cities, towns, and villages, in the several provinces of our kingdom: we have given to these representations more attention, because informed that our magistrates are convinced of the necessity of a reform in this part of the public police, and have long desired suitable laws in union with the rules of the Church, to provide for the purity of the air, without infringing, if possible, upon the rights of Archbishops, Bishops, curates, patrons, Lords, founders, &c. in the churches of our kingdom: these wishes having reached us, we think it unnecessary to defer any longer making known our intentions, and we are persuaded that our subjects will receive, with gratitude, a regulation dictated by our zeal for their preservation."

The articles which follow prohibit grave-yards in cities or towns, of which the Archbishop of Toulouse had already given an example in his diocese; and they permit no interment in churches, chapels, or cloisters, but for such persons as have been already mentioned in speaking of the decree of Parliament; and ordain besides, that even those shall not be interred except under vaults, covering a space of seventy-two square feet, built of stone, and flagged; the bodies to be placed six feet deep in the earth, under the lower pavement of the vault: they also invest municipal corporations with the right to obtain and hold, in fee simple, any grounds for new cemeteries. Thus all that could be devised in point of legislation, to do away the evils of interment in churches and towns, was at length accomplished.

The practice of intermixing the dead with the living would never have grown to such an intolerable height, though aided by all the pride of the great, all the immorality of the rich, and the desire of distinction inherent to all ranks, if the reverence for the relics of saints, and the blind belief in the power of the Church over souls after death, had not rooted in the hearts of the people a strong conviction that a grave in the cloister, the galilee, the portico, the chapel, or the aisle, was a stronghold for protection against the arch enemy, and a passport to heaven. As this superstition declined, or became modified, the practice to which it had given rise still continued and grew more and more immovable the more it was habitual. It is the same in thousands of instances to this day, even where the original motive is forgotten, and such is the force of custom, that it continues in cemeteries consecrated by the vicinity of particular churches to so great a degree, that the peace of the grave is continually violated, to crowd new tenants into the spot hallowed to them in life by pious associations. In the year 1777, Mons. Lenoir, minister of police, devised the entire abolition of the cemetery of the Innocents, by clearing out its charnels and pits, and removing the remains into the catacombs, (¹) or

(¹) The CATACOMBS were formed by the removal of bodies from the different church yards and burial places within the walls of Paris, more especially from the cemeteries of the Innocents, St. Eustache, and St. Etienne des Grès. Immense quarries, that had been worked for ages, to obtain stone, of which the greater part of Paris had been constructed, and which even extended under a great portion of the southern Faubourgs, were devoted to the reception of these remains. The ceremony of consecration was performed on the seventh of April, 1786, and on the same night

quarries which had been worked from time imme- morial, under the southern part of Paris. This great design was not prosecuted until ten years after ; (¹) it has, however, been fully accomplished, and the salubrity of Paris sensibly promoted.

the removal of the bodies commenced. The bones were borne to their destination by torch light, in funeral cars, followed by priests, chaunting the service for the dead ; they were carefully cleaned and arranged under the direction of M. Héricart de Thouret. In the principal gallery, the large bones of the arms, legs, and thighs, are closely and neatly piled together, intersected by rows of sculls, behind which are thrown the smaller bones. In the other rooms they are variously, but always tastefully arranged. The entrance to this palace of the dead, is at a short distance from the barrière d'Enfer, by a winding staircase of ninety steps. Visitors must be accompanied by a guide, and provide themselves with wax tapers. After proceeding about a mile, they arrive at the vestibule of the Catacombs. On each side the entrance is a Tus- can pilaster ; and over the door is the following inscription, in Latin :—" Beyond these bounds rest the dead, awaiting the joyful hope of immortality." This gallery conducts to rooms containing chapels, in one of which are deposited the remains of the victims of 1792 ; another called *Tombeau de la Revolution*, is dedicated to the reception of the bones of those who fell during the early stages of that era. A faint mouldering smell pervades these caverns, but not to any unpleasant degree. It is certain that the remains of more than three millions of human beings are entombed here ; some writers have estimated them at six millions. In one apartment, Mons. Thouret has formed a collection of the fossil remains, mineral productions, and spars, which these quarries afford ; in another, he has scientifically arranged an assemblage of diseased bones and sculls, of remarkable structure. Having quitted the Catacombs, the stranger follows a black line, traced on the roof, which conducts him to another staircase, six hundred yards East of the road to Orleans, which he had crossed under ground.

(') On the subject of burying grounds, and the poisonous

In 1790, the National Assembly passed a law, commanding all towns and villages to discontinue the use of their old burial places, and to form others at a distance from their habitations. An imperial de-effluvia arising from dead bodies, no better authority can be cited than Fourcroy. His two memoirs on the disinterment of the burying grounds of the Innocents, in Paris, in 1786 and 1787, may be found in the *Annales de Chimie*, vol. 5, p. 154, and vol. 8. p. 17. The following is faithfully translated from his first memoir :—

" We had a strong desire to satisfy ourselves, by experiment, what was the nature of the destructive air given off from decaying bodies. We had no opportunity in consequence of no interments having taken place during the three preceding years, and *the last deposit, in* 1782, *had passed the period when the poisonous evolution of gas takes place from the abdomen.* In vain we endeavoured to induce the grave diggers to procure us an examination of this elastic fluid in other burying grounds. *They uniformly refused,*—declaring that it was only by an unlucky accident they interfered with dead bodies in that dangerous state. The horrible odour and the poisonous activity of this fluid announce to us, that if it is mingled, as there is no reason to doubt, with hydrogenous and azotic gas, holding sulphur and phosphorous in solution, ordinary and known products of putrefaction, it may contain also another deleterious vapour, whose nature has hitherto escaped philosophical research, while its terrible action upon life is too strikingly evinced. Perhaps it belongs to another order of bodies, to a substance more attenuated and fugacious than the bases of the known elastic fluids ; and that in this view the constituent matter of this gas operates. Be this as it may, the grave diggers know, that there is nothing in the burial grounds really dangerous for them but the vapour disengaged from the abdomen of carcases when that cavity bursts. They have further remarked that this vapour does not always strike them with asphyxia ; for if they are at some distance from the corpse which emits it, it affects them only with a slight vertigo ; a feeling of a disagreeable kind, and weakness and nausea, which are of secree was issued in 1804, ordering high ground to be chosen for cemeteries, and every corpse to be interred at a depth of at least five or six feet. Another decree of 1811, still in force, ordained a company of undertakers, to whom the whole business of interment is consigned, who have arranged funerals into six classes, and established a tariff of expenses. The cemeteries of Paris are four in number, Père-la-Chaise, Montmarte, Vaugirard, and Mont Parnasse.

The CIMETIÈRE DU PERE LA CHAISE occupies a tract of high and sloping ground to the north-east of Paris. It derives its name from the confessor of

veral hours duration. These symptoms are followed by loss of appetite, debility, and trembling, all in consequence of a subtle poison, that fortunately is developed in only one stage of decomposition. May it not be credited, that to this septic miasma is owing the diseases to which persons are exposed who live in the neighbourhood of burying grounds, sewers, and in short all places where animal substances, in heaps, undergo spontaneous decomposition? May we not be permitted to suppose that a poison so terrible as to cause the sudden extinction of animal life, when it escapes pure and concentrated from its focus, or place of production, may, when received and diluted in the atmosphere, retain activity enough to produce on the nervous and sensible solids of animals, an operation capable of benumbing their functions and deranging their motions? Since we have witnessed the terror which this dangerous poison excites among the labourers in cemeteries,—since we have seen in a great number of them a paleness of face, and all the symptoms of a slow poison, it would be more unsafe to deny the effects of these exhalations upon the neighbouring inhabitants than to multiply and exaggerate complaints, as has been done, by an abusive application of the discoveries by physics upon air and the other elastic fluids."

Louis XIV. who occupied a splendid mansion on its site—a country house of the Jesuits during one hundred and fifty subsequent years. This burial ground was consecrated in 1804, and on the twenty-first of May of that year, the first corpse was interred within its walls. In the *fosses communes* the poor are gratuitously interred, in coffins placed side by side, and covered with quick lime and soil, to the depth of four feet and a half. Any person may purchase ground. Amongst the celebrated characters whose ashes repose here, are Baron Cuvier, Casimir Périer, and Benjamin Constant. Here also may be found monuments to the memory of the Duc de Laval Montmorency, the medical professor Hallé, Bernardin de St. Pierre, Grétry, Delille, Chenier, Varney, Brougniard, Talma, Mademoiselle Raucourt, Mazurier, Volney, Labbé-doyère, Macdonald, Beaumarchais, Madame Cottin, Marshal Lefèvre, Marshal Massena, Marshal Suchet, Marshal Ney, General Foy, the Marchioness de Beauharnois, sister-in-law of the Empress Josephine, Molière, Lafontaine, De Sèze, David, the Abbé Sicard, and Madame Blanchard, the aeronant, who perished in consequence of her balloon taking fire, 1819; a picturesque monument, of gothic architecture, to the right on entering, near the Jews' burial ground, contains the ashes of Abelard and Heloisa. This sepulchre was constructed from the ruins of the celebrated Abbey of the Paraclet.

The CIMETIÈRE MONTMARTRE lies to the north of Paris, and was the first opened after the suppression of the burial grounds in the city. The irregularity of the site bestows an air of picturesque beauty upon this cemetery. The most prominent monument is a lofty stone obelisk to the memory of the Duchesse de Montmorency. Here also are interred the families of Voyer d'Argenson, d'Arguesseau, de Segur, and Sevestre. Pigulle and St. Lambert were also buried here.

The CIMETIÈRE DE VAUGIRARD, near the barrière de Sevres, is only remarkable as containing the remains of Lavalette, Mlle. Clairon, and La Harpe.

In the CIMETIÈRE DE MONT-PARNASSE are monuments to the memory of the Marquis d'Arguesseau (the last of that illustrious family), the Duchess de Gesvres (the last of the Duguesclins), and the Comte de Montmorency Laval.

The French Government has therefore shown itself pre-eminently attentive to the health, and, consequently, to the happiness of its members. Commissions were issued—enquiries instituted—laws enacted—royal decrees published, and well arranged plans formed and executed. The remains of those who had long lain mouldering in their tombs have been carefully removed from the interior of cities, and respectfully and securely deposited, and mortuaries have been fixed and consecrated for those who follow so far distant from "the busy hum of men" as not to molest or endanger the survivors; whilst in almost every other country (¹) the putrefactive process emanating from those who have gone to their last homes is allowed to accumulate in the very midst of the habitations of the living, and to form the nuclei of increase, if not the origin, of the most malignant diseases.

This important subject engaged the authorities of New York in the beginning of the present century. The Board of Health of that city, in 1806, appointed a Committee, to report on measures necessary to secure the health of the inhabitants, and a prohibition of interment within the city was afterwards formally determined upon. I have taken the following extract from the work of Dr. Pascalis, before referred to, and regret that his publication had not fallen into my hands at an earlier period. The extract is from the report of the Commissioners to the Board of Health, drawn up by a Dr. Miller:—

" The interments of dead bodies within the city *ought to be prohibited.* A vast mass of decaying animal matter, produced by the superstition of interring dead bodies near the churches, and which has been accumulating for a long lapse of time, is now deposited in many of the most populous parts of the city. It is impossible that such a quantity of these animal remains, even if placed at the greatest depth of interment commonly practised, should

(¹) Ireland and Denmark are named by Dr. Piattoli as exceptions. It appears that " a pestilential fever raged in Dublin during the summer of 1740, which was traced to the exhalations from church yards, which, by authority, were removed out of the city."

continue to be inoffensive and safe. It is difficult, if not impracticable, to determine to what distance around, the matter extricated during the progress of putrefaction, may spread; and by pervading the ground, tainting the waters, and perhaps emitting noxious exhalations into the atmosphere, do great mischief. But if it should be decided still to persist in the practice of interments within the city, it ought to be judged necessary to order the envelopment of the bodies in some species of calcareous earth, either quick lime or chalk. The present burial grounds might serve extremely well for plantations of grove and forest trees, and thereby, instead of remaining receptacles of putrefying matter and hot-beds of miasmata, might be rendered useful and ornamental to the city. This growing evil must be corrected at some period, for it is increasing and extending, by daily aggregation, to a mass already very large, and the sooner it is arrested the less violence will be done to the feeling and habits of our fellow citizens."

Dr. Piattoli, in his work on the " Dangers of Interment," had derived much information from the writings of several eminent French physicians who preceded him, without making any acknowledgment of the sources by which he had been so liberally supplied. Vicq. d'Azyr, in his " Remarks" upon the Italian work, has supplied the omission, " in order to render to the French nation the honour legitimately due to it; and proving, by extracts from the writers adverted to, that to them we are indebted for the first elements of reform upon the subject on which they treat." In justice to those authors I shall now give from the " Remarks" a general outline of their labours.

Dr. HAGUENOT, of the University of Montpelier, is the first among the moderns who strenuously exerted himself against the custom of burying in churches. Dr. MARET, Secretary to the Academy of Dijon, published upon the same subject in 1774, and Dr. NAVIER, of Chalons, highly deserving the reputation he obtained, demonstrated the pernicious effects of precipitate exhumations.

First, Dr. Haguenot had long observed with extreme pain the custom of interment in churches, which prevailed, not only in Montpelier, but also in the rest of France. The dreadful consequences of the practice which passed under his own observation, confirmed the opinions he had formed. He was restrained from publishing his views from apprehensions that he should not succeed in convincing others, but the following catastrophe determined him at last to break a silence which, if prolonged, would have become culpable :—

On the 17th August, 1744, at six o'clock in the evening, Wm. Boudou, a layman, was buried in one of the common graves of the parish church of Notre Dame, at Montpelier ; Peter Balsalgette, a street porter, was employed as grave digger ; he had scarcely descended into the grave when he was seen to be convulsed, and he soon fell down motionless ;

Joseph Sarrau offered to draw out the unhappy man,
—he descended, holding by a rope; he had scarcely
seized the dress of the street-porter when he became
insensible—he was drawn up half dead,—in a short
time he recovered his senses, but he experienced a
kind of vertigo and numbness, the forerunners of convulsions and faintings, which displayed themselves a
quarter of an hour afterwards; during the night he
felt weak—his whole body trembled, and he experienced palpitations which were removed by bleed-
ing and cordials; he was for a long time pale and
emaciated, and throughout the city bore the name
of the " *Resuscitated.*"

This sad event did not prevent John Molinier
from exposing himself with a similar zeal, to save
the street-porter,—but scarcely had he entered the
grave, than feeling himself suffocating, he gave
signs to be drawn up and supported,—he came up
so weak and so faint that a moment's delay would
have been fatal.   Robert Molinier, brother of the
last, stronger and more robust, thought he might
brave the danger, and gratify the kind feeling by
which he was influenced; but he fell a victim to his
temerity, and died as soon as he had reached the
bottom of the grave.   This tragical scene was terminated by the death of Charles Balsalgette, brother
of the street-porter, who remained in the grave.
As he was obliged to arrange the body of Robert
Molinier, he stayed longer than he ought, and he
was forced to get out.   He thought he could safely
descend a second time, by placing between his teeth

a handkerchief, dipped in Hungary water; this precaution was useless—he staggered to the ladder, and used every effort to ascend, but, at the third step, he fell back lifeless.

Notwithstanding the most earnest entreaties by priests and others, no one could afterwards be found willing to risk the danger of withdrawing from the grave the bodies of the victims—they were taken out by hooks, and their clothes exhaled a disgusting odour.

Dr. Haguenot was commissioned to examine and report upon the nature and qualities of this destructive vapour. With this intention, he went several times to the church of Notre Dame, and made the following experiments :—

First experiment.—Dr. Haguenot had the grave opened,—a very fetid odour issued from it, which impregnated linen, thread, even glass bottles and clothes, with a cadaverous odour.

Second experiment.—Lighted paper, chips, and tarred rope, placed at the opening of the grave, were entirely extinguished.

Third experiment.—Cats and dogs thrown into this grave, were strongly convulsed, and expired in two or three minutes,—birds, in some seconds.

Fourth experiment.—The mephitic vapour from the grave was collected and preserved in bottles, and six weeks afterwards submitted to the same experiments; it had lost none of its destructive properties.

These experiments were made in the presence of

a Committee of scientific gentlemen, and demonstrate the danger arising from cadaverous vapours, and consequently that of interment in churches. With the view of convincing those yet doubting, Dr. Haguenot adds the following considerations :—

Air, to support animal life, ought to possess all its activity. Vapours from wine, in a state of fermentation, from bodies, in a state of putrefaction, &c. deprive the air of its respirable property. He attributed the malignity of the small pox, which had proved very destructive that same year at Montpelier, to emanations from dead bodies.

He disapproves of *the scandalous, and at the same time dangerous custom of carrying the remains of unburied bodies, bones, often surrounded with flesh, partially decomposed,* to places called *reservoirs,* to make room for new bodies, and thus to render graves the source of perpetual gain.

Dr. Haguenot observes that the exhalations of animal putrefaction have two equally pernicious effects. First, to kill, instantaneously, animals exposed to their action. ([1]) Second, by mixing with,

([1]) In the effects of these exhalations we may obtain an explanation of certain phenomena which some authors have considered as miraculous. Gregory, of Tours, relates that a robber, having dared to enter the tomb of St. Helius, this prelate retained him, and prevented him from getting out. The same author informs us that a poor man, not having a stone to cover the place in which one of his children had been buried, took away one which closed the opening of an old tomb, in which rested, without doubt, says Gregory of Tours, the remains of some holy personage. The unhappy father was immediately and simultaneously struck dumb, blind, and deaf. These facts may be attributed to mephitic vapours.

and thus infecting the air, to produce very fatal, and even pestilential diseases, which arise from the injurious emanations, and which must be carefully distinguished from diseases of an epidemic nature.

We may, it is said, carefully seal the stones and stop up all the openings through which this vapour might escape, but, setting aside the difficulty even if we wished to accomplish it, we should only put off the danger, and even render it greater. Gasses, strongly concentrated and pent up, only become the more destructive.

Dr. Haguenot afterwards shows that the civil and ecclesiastical laws have always forbidden interment in churches,—that at first cemeteries were chosen in country places, at a distance from towns—that the custom of inhumation in temples had gradually prevailed, but not without having several times been abolished, and that it is countenanced only because people have wished to confer honours upon certain Princes and Pontiffs—because ambitious laymen have offered considerable sums to enjoy this distinction; and finally, because the clergy have been more willing to relax the discipline of the Church than to sacrifice pecuniary advantages.

Second, Dr. Maret points out the evils which may be produced by animal exhalations. A mild catarrhal fever, he says, prevailed at Saulieu, in Burgundy; the body of a very fat man was buried in the parish church of St. Saturnin; twenty-three days afterwards a grave was opened by the side of the former to bury a woman there, who had died of the same disease. A very fetid odour immediately filled the church, and affected all those who entered. In letting down the body, a rope slipped, by which the coffin was shaken —a discharge of sanies followed, the odour of which greatly annoyed the assistants ;—of one hundred and seventy persons who entered the church, from the opening of the grave until the interment, one hundred and forty-nine were attacked with a malignant putrid fever, which had some resemblance to the reigning catarrhal fever, but the nature and intensity of the symptoms left no doubt that the malignity was owing *to the infection of the cathedral.* (¹)

Dr. Maret states that the custom of burying in churches is posterior to the year 509, because it was in that same year that Pope Marcellus obtained from the Senate permission to establish a cemetery at Rome. The prohibition to bury in churches, contained in one of the statutes of Charlemagne, proves also the antiquity of this custom. The same

(¹) July, 1773.—*Letters from Paris give the following further particulars of the accident that happened on the opening a grave* in the body of the church of St. Saturnin, on the 20th of April, at Saulieu :—of one hundred and twenty young persons, of both sexes, who were assembled to receive their first communion, all but six fell dangerously ill, together with the Curé, the grave diggers, and sixty-six other persons. The illness with which they were seized is described to be a putrid verminous fever, accompanied with an hæmorrhage, eruption, and inflammation. As the persons who were affected, principally dwelt near the church, and the cause being known, a stop was happily put to the contagion, but not before it had carried off eighteen, among whom were the Curé and the vicar.—(From Dodsley's *Annual Register.)*

H

law was in vigour at the commencement of the twelfth century, since the mausoleum of Regnault I. Count of Burgundy, was erected, in 1057, in the portico of the church of St. Stephen, at Besançon, and the body of Eudes I. Duke of Burgundy, was deposited in 1102, under the front gate of the entrance of the Abbey of Citeaux, which he had founded.

M. Maret, in a letter to the editor of the Journal Encyclopédique, in 1775, states that the curate of Arnay-le-duc, after having breathed the infected air arising from the dead body of one of his parishioners when he was performing the funeral rites, contracted a putrid disease, which had reduced him to the last extremity.

A nobleman of a village, two miles from Nantes, having died, it was thought proper, with a view of giving a more distinguished place to the coffin, to remove several others, and among them that of one of his relations, who had died three months before ; a most fetid odour spread through the church : five of the assistants died a little after. Four persons who had removed the coffins, also died, and six curates, who were present at the ceremony, had nearly perished.

Third, Dr. Navier published his work in 1775. He cites several instances of accidents which happened after the opening of different graves, and the breaking up of several cemeteries. He thinks that four years are not sufficient for the destruction of a body inhumed, and relates that he had examined three bodies disinterred; one had been buried twenty, another eleven, and the third seven years; all the three were yet covered with flesh, in a state of putrefaction.

Dr. Navier inveighs with reason against the practice of *charnel houses*, in which the remnants of carcases and bones, still covered with putrefying flesh, are exposed, and the odour of which infects both churches and cities. These dangers would not be apprehended if the barbarous and unreasonable custom of burying, in the midst of the living, thousands of the dead, which convey the germ of putrid and malignant diseases of every kind, were abolished.

Dr. Navier disapproves of the custom of planting trees in cemeteries; their roots, he says, throw obstacles in the way of the grave diggers, and frequently do great damage to the walls of churches; their branches, also, are very injurious, by retaining the fetid vapours, so that the air cannot circulate with so much facility as when the cemetery is open to every wind—which is a situation of all others the most advantageous. It is very true, says Dr. Navier, that according to Dr. Priestley, vegetation absorbs a certain quantity of fixed air; and although the truth of this is placed beyond all doubt, might it not invariably be said that the renewal of the air is the surest and simplest means of restoring its purity?

I have thus supplied, from the " Remarks" of Vicq. d'Azyr, the information furnished by the predecessors of Dr. Piattoli.

I shall now state the views entertained by different writers upon the nature, products, and effects of animal decomposition ; commencing with copious extracts from the work of Dr. Piattoli, before cited, and afterwards submitting my own views upon the subject. The description and state of the burying grounds of the metropolis, and the abuses of interment, will then follow ; and the work will be concluded with a few general observations.

FACTS AND EXPERIMENTS DEMONSTRATING THE DANGERS OF INHUMATION IN CHURCHES AND WITHIN CITIES.

Fermentation is an action peculiar to vegetable and animal substances, which experience has shown would soon degenerate into putrefaction, if an organic power, the nature of which is unknown, did not suspend its operations. ([1])

As fermentation goes on, elementary air is disengaged ; its free communication with atmospheric air gives all its properties to the latter ; in its development and rarefaction it diminishes the adher-

([1]) The putrefaction of dead bodies presents different phenomena in different climates. A. Marcellinus assures us that the dead are preserved longer in Persia than in Rome and the rest of Europe. Chaulin, however, says that the dead bodies of the Persians putrify very rapidly, and Calmet pretends that the Israelites learned from the Persians not to delay the burial of their dead.—(*Diss. de Fun. Heb.*) Ortesius (*Vide Theatr. Ort.*) speaks of certain islands in which the dead do not putrify.

ence of the parts of the body in which it is operating, and disengaging itself, it carries with it the most subtle, oleaginous or inflammable molecules, which then remain suspended in the atmosphere.

We all know how much the different modifications of the air influence the animal economy and the health of man. This element continually surrounds us within and without; its action incessantly balances that of the fluids which tend to become rarefied, and to be decomposed; it increases the resistance of the solids; it insinuates itself into our humours, either by mixing with our aliments, or by penetrating through the pores of the membrane which lines the lungs after having combined with the halitus of the bronchi.

It is equally certain that the qualities of the atmosphere depend upon a great number of causes which more or less concur to preserve its natural properties, or to supply it with factitious ones; to render it light or dense, pure or charged with heterogenous principles, elastic or rare. The smallest insects, as well as the globes above us; meteors, seasons, the temperature of different climates, the number of inhabitants in a country, the practice of the arts, the operations of commerce, all act upon the air, and produce changes in it.

Among the different modifications of this fluid, there are some which more closely concern us, either because they immediately influence the respiration, and the emanations of bodies, or because they prepare our organs to receive, in a more sensible manner, the deleterious impressions of certain pernicious causes, the effects of which, although they may not be always sudden, are not less fatal.([1]) The atmosphere, when hot and rarified, necessarily loses a part of its elasticity,—weighing less in respect to the elementary air, and at the same time more impure and thick, on account of the heterogeneous matters with which it is surcharged, it becomes more suffocating. If humidity be joined to the other bad qualities of the air, it becomes more and more poisonous.

The action of the air upon the solids being diminished, their fibres relax, their resistance diminishes, their more volatile particles fly off, and the internal motion is accelerated. The internal moving powers increase in proportion to the diminution of the external powers, and fermentation, which soon passes into putrescency, is a necessary consequence of it.

When heated air acts upon dead bodies, that is to say, upon bodies which being deprived of their natural heat, experience the action of external heat, they soon increase in volume; the cellular tissue of the vessels swell, and putrefaction is rapid.

Living bodies also are very susceptible of every impression made upon them by the air. They are even in danger of putrefaction in periods of increased heat combined with moisture.

([1]) HYER. DAVID. GAUB.—*Instit. Patholog.* § 429, *et seq. Vide* M.MARET. " *Sur l' usage où l' en est d' enterrer les morts dans les églises et dans l' enceinte des villes.*" A Dijon, chez Causse, 1773.

The air, loaded with putrid emanations, would necessarily become deadly if the different exhalations which arose from certain bodies did not correct those emanations, and if the winds did not dissipate the principles of corruption. There will be every thing to fear if the infected air is stagnant, if it is seldom renewed, especially if it has been respired too long a time. Experience, besides, has often shown that the infection of the air exposes us to the most alarming dangers, (¹) and that diseases of a fatal nature, such as malignant, putrid, and exanthematous fevers are sometimes the dreadful consequences of it.(²)

Enlightened by these principles, we shall easily comprehend why all subterranean places, low and marshy places, and places surrounded by mountains and thick forests, are so insalubrious,—why maladies are so frequent, and almost all of them malignant, in places where the air is always impregnated

(¹) *Haud aliud vitium exitialius est,* inquit Gaubius, loc. cit. § 438, *quam quod diuturnà stagnatione in locis undique occlusis—contrahit aer, cum nullâ ventilatione renovatur. Torpore enim veluti putrescens, qui vitæ cibus fuerat, velox fit venenum vitæ non minus quam flamma inimicissimum.* Vide et. § 439.

(²) The Abbe Rozier, in his *Observations de Physique,* &c. tome 1, relates that a person at Marseilles had ordered a piece of land to be dug up for a plantation of trees during the plague of 1720, many dead bodies had been buried in this place; the workmen had scarcely commenced their labours when three of them were suffocated without the possibility of recovery, and the others with difficulty escaped.

with fetid particles.([1]) The properties of the air thus known, show why the workmen engaged in certain trades, become pale and enfeebled. ([2]) We see also why army, hospital, and prison fevers make such dreadful ravages.

Lancisi makes several reflections upon the subject on which we are treating, in his work upon the dangers to which the neighbourhood of marshes is exposed. ([3]) Ramazzini assures us that those who dig graves do not live long ; the vapours which they respire soon destroy them. ([4]) The same author, in a well known work upon the diseases of artizans, mentions all the diseases by which those who empty cess-pools and sewers, are ordinarily attacked. Mons. Paré saw, at Paris, five young and robust men die in a ditch which they were to have emptied, in the Fauxbourg Saint Honoré. ([5]) George Hanneus relates a fact nearly similar, which took place at Rendsburg, in the Duchy of Holstein ; four persons died in a well which had been a long time shut up, and the waters of which were corrupted. A young child also was suffocated at Florence, in a pit of manure, into which it had fallen ; another person, who ran to its assistance, also perished ; and

([1]) The Romans compelled a certain class of workmen to build their shops out of the walls or in the extremities of the city.—ZACCH. *Quæst. med. leg.* l, 5, *t.* 4. *sec.* 7.

([2]) RAMAZZ. *de morb. artif.* cap. 17, &c.

([3]) De nox. palud. effluv. passim.

([4]) RAMAZZ. loc. cit.

([5]) L. 22, c. 3.

a dog thrown in was suffocated. Sennert speaks
of a disease called *Febris Hungarica*, which broke
out in the armies of the Emperor, and spread like a
contagious disease throughout all Europe. This
sort of fever often happens in camps, when troops
remain a long time in an unhealthy situation during
the summer. Dr. Pringle observed that the same
thing happens in hospitals badly managed and very
full of patients, as well as in prisons which are too
much crowded.([1])

Haller, in his Physiology, has given an extract of
all that has been written upon this subject.([2])
Tissol, in his " *Avis au Peuple*," has also presented these objects in a very striking point of view;
he complains of the dangerous custom of interment
in the interior of churches.([3])

We all know that animal exhalations, and especially those which arise from a dead body, in the
process of putrefaction, are very afflicting and very
dangerous. ([4])

When in a living subject any part tends to putrefaction, because the humours are stagnant, or leave
the vessels destined to contain them, the putrid affections are very easily communicated to the neighbouring parts. The blood of a woman, attacked
with a malignant fever, spread so unpleasant an
odour, that the surgeon and all the assistants fainted.

([1]) HUXHAM. *Observ. de morb. epidem.*

([2]) L. 8, sect. 3, § 12, et seq.

([3]) Tom. 1, c. 1, § 6.

([4]) HOFFMAN. *Dissert. de Putred. doct. Haller, c.* 1.

Old ulcers and cancers, when open, are not less pernicious. (¹)

Diodorus, of Sicily, speaks of pestilential diseases which were produced by the putrefaction of different substances. Egypt is ravaged almost every year by malignant fevers; and from that country the small pox has spread through all the earth. The waters of the Nile, according to some writers, after remaining some time in the fields they inundate, leave there an immense number of aquatic insects which, as they putrify, exhale pestilential miasmata. Forestus and John Wolf, relate that several fish, thrown dead upon the shore, occasioned a very dreadful epidemic. The putrefaction of locusts, in Ethiopia, often occasions epidemic diseases. Those on the sea coast suffer much from

(¹) Dr. Louis, in his work " De la certitude des signes de la mort," 1783, observes, " that the malignity of putrefaction resides in particles so subtle, that they may occasion death by the impression which they instantaneously produce upon the vital principle. A cadaverous effluvium has often produced this effect. It is not necessary that the putrid, malignant, or poisonous substances should mix with our fluids, to exercise over us their malignant influence. We find in Paré a convincing proof of this; he says that in uncovering the bed of a person seized with the plague, to dress a bubo, which this patient had in the groin, and two very considerable ulcers, placed on the abdomen, he was attacked by so fetid an odour from the discharge of these abscesses, that he instantly fell to the ground, as if he were dead; his senses having returned, he arose, but he was obliged to hold the bed-post, in order to support himself. It appeared to him that the house was turning round—he felt neither pain nor sickness—his strength gradually returned, and he sneezed nine or ten times so violently that his nose bled.

the putrefaction of whales, thrown upon the beach. Paré informs us, that in his time, the putrefaction of a whale produced a pestilence in Tuscany, and Lancisi writes, that the exhalations from a putrefying ox killed an unfortunate traveller, in the environs of Pessara. Lucan speaks of an epidemic which occasioned dreadful ravages in the army of Pompey, near Durazzo, and which was caused by the putrefaction of the horses which had been killed and left upon the field. Ammianus Marcellinus also makes mention of a great desolation in the camp of Constantine the Great, through the same imprudence. How often, indeed, have the numerous bodies, scattered over the field of battle, after a very sanguinary engagement, been the occasion of disease and death! Aristotle advised Alexander to remove from Arbela immediately after the defeat of Darius, to avoid the pestilential influences of the dead. France was frequently exposed to dreadful pestilences, from the tenth to the sixteenth century; and history informs us, that during this period, she was often ravaged by civil wars and dreadful famines. Provinces then sometimes remained uncultivated, and their inhabitants crowded into cities, where, by the sudden and excessive increase of population, they were reduced to the most distressing privations. Almost all long sieges, in which much blood has been shed, are accompanied by fevers and fatal diseases. The war of the Swedes, in the seventeenth century, occasioned a terrible pestilence which desolated Poland. Cruel and obstinate wars have had the same effect in Hungary, in Austria, in Syria, and in many other kingdoms,—the same thing has frequently happened in Asia. Paré relates, that in 1572, a pestilential fever spread nearly ten leagues round in Guienne, occasioned by the putrid exhalations of a pit, into which several dead bodies had been thrown, two months before.

Emanations of this kind are very penetrating, they alter the mass of the humours and *produce violent diseases, or render dangerous those which happen, or to which persons are predisposed.* Head aches, paroxysms of fever, nervous diseases, convulsions, even miscarriages, have sometimes been the effects of them. Ramazzini relates that a sexton, having descended into a grave to strip a corpse, which had recently been deposited there, was suffocated and fell dead upon the spot. [1]

At Riom, in Auvergne, the earth was removed from an ancient cemetery, with the view of embellishing the city. In a short time after an epidemic

[1] M. Berard relates that the body of a very fat person had been buried about a foot and a half deep, so that only a foot of ground and a stone, seven or eight inches thick, covered it. In a short time, the vapours which arose were so offensive, that it was rendered necessary to disinter the body. Three grave diggers undertook the work; two, attacked with nausea and vomiting, quitted the work, but the third, who determined to finish it, died ten days after.

We read in the Journal of the Abbé Rozier, that a grave digger, working at the cemetery of Montmorency, struck a dead body which had been interred a year before, and that he was immediately overpowered by the vapours which arose from it.—*Observ. Phys. t.* 1.

disease arose, which carried off many persons, particularly of the poorer class, and the mortality was especially prevalent in the neighbourhood of the cemetery. Six years before, a similar event had caused an epidemic in Ambert, a small town in the same province. *Such a train of facts leaves no doubt of the infection produced by the exhalations of dead bodies.*

Air confined, heated, and deprived of its elasticity, is of itself dangerous from whatever body it proceeds, even if it results from the perspiration of persons in the best state of health. If the perspiration of the sick, and the exhalations of dead animals diffuse poisonous vapours; if each of these properties by itself can produce the most fatal consequences—to what dangers may we not be exposed by interment in churches, where the air is impregnated with the most dangerous materials, and where all the causes of contagion, elsewhere divided, are found combined? ([1])

The atmosphere in churches is ordinarily moist and heavy—it acquires those qualities from the emanations of those who there assemble. The mixture of sepulchral exhalations which necessarily

([1]) Chitelius has proved in his work, *de ant. fun. rit. posit.* 2, § 5, that the air in a church, charged with the vapours that arise from tombs, readily contracts pernicious qualities in proportion to the extent of the place and the number of dead bodies in it—in addition to which, that the ground in which dead bodies have been left for a long time to putrify is so saturated with fetid particles, that whenever tombs are opened, accidents are likely to happen.— (Vide KECKERMANN Sist. 1. 1, c. 3.)

penetrate through the layers of earth by which the bodies are covered, cannot fail to become injurious in a place where every thing tends to concentrate the deleterious vapours. There is another cause which increases the putridity of the air contained in churches, and that is, the necessity of frequently opening the tombs to inter in them new bodies, or to remove those which have been there deposited, when the ground is not sufficient for the burials. In these two cases they are obliged to be kept open a considerable time. The atmosphere is then charged with the noxious vapours from bodies which are only half decomposed, or the putrefaction of which is recent.

The only remedy for evils which necessarily result from so pernicious a custom is the renewal of the air, whereas it is almost always stationary in churches; and, if even a portion of this fluid experiences any motion in them, the whole mass is never entirely displaced.

These expressions may perhaps appear exaggerated—they may be attributed to a fear of contagion altogether imaginary; the following authenticated facts will remove all doubt upon the subject :—

We learn from HALLER, that a church was infected by the exhalations of a single body, twelve years after burial—and that this corpse occasioned a very dangerous disease in a whole convent. (¹)

(¹) In the works of Pennecher upon embalments, we read that the vapour of a tomb caused a malignant fever to an unhappy grave digger.—(GOCKEL, cent. 11, obs. 33.)

RAULIN relates, that the opening of a corpse occasioned a dreadful epidemic in the plain of Armagnac.([1]) Sensitive and nervous persons frequently became ill, and fainted after having been attacked with cadaverous exhalations when walking along a cemetery. ([2])

Workmen were digging vaults in the church of St. Eustache, in Paris, which compelled them to displace some bodies, and to place those which came afterwards in a vault which had been long closed. Some children who went to catechism in the place were taken ill there ; several adults also were similarly affected. Dr. Ferret, Regent of the Faculty of Paris, was directed to report upon it. He found the respiration of the patients difficult, the action of the brain disordered, the heart beating irregularly, and, in some, convulsive movements of the arms and legs.

A place, upon which a convent for nuns of St. Génevieve at Paris had been situated, was afterwards built upon and converted into shops. All those who lived in them first, especially very young persons, exhibited nearly the same symptoms as those above mentioned ; which were attributed, with justice, to the exhalations of dead bodies interred in this ground.

But why seek elsewhere for examples of that

([1]) *Ibid.* RAULIN *de Médec.*

([2]) These and the following examples are from HABBERMANN. *Dissert. de optimo sepeliendi usu. Thes. publ. propug. &c. Vindob.* 1772.

which passes daily under our own review ?   If we were disposed to collect here all the observations of those who have preceded us, we should have innumerable proofs of what we advance : owing to the small number of the learned, or of those capable of transmitting to posterity the fatal effects of interments in churches and cities, or rather on account of the respect with which the custom of burying in temples has always been regarded among us, epidemic diseases, which have from time to time depopulated our cities, have often been attributed to other causes.   The smallest district preserves the recollection of some similar events : and, if in several countries, it is in contemplation to re-establish the ancient common cemeteries beyond towns, the strongest and most influential motives have given origin to the undertaking.

It is known that the inhabitants of Rome repaired with the greatest reluctance to the church of St. Lorenzo, in Lucina, in which there were almost daily burials, and frequent exhumations.   It is the same also in several other extensive parishes in different quarters of the city.

Nearly twenty years ago, the small pox prevailed as an epidemic at Rome.   The number of the dead was so considerable, that the civil and ecclesiastical powers united to prevent interment in parish churches ; that of St. Mary, in Cosmedia, at a distance from the city, became the place of sepulchre ; there all the dead were carried, and when the epidemic had ceased, they re-paved the church, renewed

the plaster floors a foot in depth, and they ceased
to perform divine service there, until they could
satisfy themselves that the dead were entirely consumed. It was not until after they had taken these
precautions, that they recommenced in that church
the celebration of the holy offices. (¹)

It would be unjust to affirm, that the Government ought to wait for the existence of these evils
before it had recourse to precautions at all times
wise and necessary. The dangerous effects of
putrid exhalations shew themselves more promptly
in individuals exposed to them of a disposition
favourable to their development;(²) but on all occa-

(¹) At Palermo they used the same precautions in the dreadful
plague of 1625 and 1626—and also at Modena in 1630. *Vide*
MURATORI in his Traité de la manière de se préserver de la Peste.

(²) " When Caspar Hauser passed on one occasion, in the
autumn of 1828, near St. John's church yard, in the vicinity of
Nuremberg, the smell of the dead bodies, of which his companion
had no perception, affected him so powerfully, that he was seized
with an ague, and began to shudder. The ague was soon succeeded by a feverish heat, which at length caused a violent perspiration, by which his linen was thoroughly wetted. When he
returned towards the city-gate he said he felt better, yet he complained that his sight was obscured thereby. What would have
been the effect produced upon this being, of so delicate a nervous
susceptibility, had he passed by some of the crowded burial places,
many of which are in the most thickly-peopled districts of London?
Although such remarkable effects are not produced upon people in
general, yet the same gases are eliminated from the thousands of
dead bodies in London, in all stages of decomposition, which
become mixed with the air, and are breathed by the people, incorporated with their blood, and thus the very putrefactions of the
dead become part of the fluids of the living. In the case of Caspar,

I

sions, the animal economy suffers much under their influence. (¹) Putrid and malignant fevers, and periodical diseases often prevail in densely populated cities, when the remote cause of them cannot be ascertained. Is it not possible that this cause, of which we are ignorant, and which is demonstrated only by its fatal effects, is no other than the interment in cities?

We have said enough to prove the indispensable necessity of placing public cemeteries beyond cities, to justify the wise dispositions of the administration in this respect, and entirely to destroy those prejudices which have no other support than public credulity,—prejudices directly opposed to the interest of those who circulate them, and who would abandon them if they were more enlightened, and if they could calculate and foresee every thing which

a living chemical test was applied, of such exquisite sensibility, that the presence and noxious qualities of these agents were demonstrated. The difference between the effects produced upon him and upon other human beings is a difference rather of degree than of kind. The emanations are equally poisonous, equally destructive to health; but most persons are less sensitive, and therefore they are better able to withstand them than Caspar."

(¹) *Subito necat idem (vapor quem cadaverum putredo generat) dicit* HALLER *op. cit. quando aperto sepulchro, hominem percellit. Nisi necat, morbos excitat periculosos et corpora putrefacit.* LABAT. *Voyage d'Italie,* tome 4. SAUVAGES, *Effets de l'air, &c.* Physicians recommend their patients not to go into churches in the morning when they have not entirely recovered their strength—there would be too much reason to fear that they would inhale some of the corrupted particles which are more frequent and more exciting in the morning.

could be prejudicial to the health of their fellow citizens. (¹)

How can we indeed put into competition the powerful suffrage of the universal custom of all times, and of the most polished nations, with the transient complaints of a few, always prejudiced in favour of the customs of the day, utterly incapable to know their own interests—influenced by the uncertainties of opinion, and ever undecided in the choice of what is useful?

The examples just given by several Princes of Europe, justify the hope that the custom of placing cemeteries at a distance from cities will be re-established. (²) Before subjecting ourselves to the charge of innovation, we have thought proper to look into the records of antiquity, and to ascertain if the custom we wish to destroy has not been

(¹) What has been said of churches applies with equal force to cemeteries within cities,—the danger is the same. We only remedy half the evil by ceasing to bury in churches, if we establish burying places in cities. The elevation of the houses and churches, and the narrowness of streets, would be so many obstacles to the dissipation of the fetid molecules infallibly arising. Cemeteries in cities are always excessively humid. The pernicious vapours which issue from them penetrate into houses, diffuse a disagreeable odour, corrupt the food, and spoil even the springs of water.

(²) At Vienna there are no cemeteries in the vicinity of churches. The Empress Maria Theresa established a public cemetery beyond the capital.

The Chancellor, D'Aguesseau, whose name alone is an eulogy, desired to be buried in the cemetery of Auteuil.

recently introduced, and if it is not the effect of a relaxation of discipline.

To give laws to a nation is the fruit of policy and courage ; but to bring back to it ancient customs which are preferable to those recently introduced, is the work of profound wisdom, supported by inflexible fortitude. In both cases the depositaries of the public authority must shut their ears against the voice of interest and of prejudice ; their duty is to do good to their fellow-men in spite of all their opposition, and, above all, they must not hunt after light and frivolous applause. The only object they should propose to themselves to attain, ought to be —*the approbation of their country.*

The lovers of epitaphs will be pleased with the following inscriptions—they are pointed and instructive ; they were made by two celebrated physicians ;—the one was met with at Paris, in the cemetery of St. Etienne-du-Mont, upon the tomb of Simon Pierre—his son was the author of it :—

SIMON PIERRE, VIR PIUS ET PROBUS
HIC SUB DIO SEPELIRI VOLUIT,
NE MORTUUS CUIQUAM NOCERET,
QUI VIVUS OMNIBUS PROFUERAT.

The other is that of the celebrated anatomist, Verbeyen, who wished to be buried in the public cemetery at Louvain :—

PHILLIPPUS VERBEYEN,

MEDICINÆ DOCTOR ET PROFESSOR,

PARTEM SUI MATERIALEM,

HIC

IN CÆMETERIO CONDI VOLUIT,

NE TEMPLUM DEHONESTARET

AUT NOCIVIS HALITIBUS INFICERET.

I cannot refrain from inserting in this place the following beautiful epitaph, which I met with on a pedestrian tour from Paris to Brussels, in 1835; it was in the village church yard of La Chapelle-en-Serval, near the birth place of *Jean Jacques Rousseau* :—

" A la mémoire de Messire Jacques Marie Massicot, leur pasteur, les habitans de la Chapelle-en-Serval reconnaissans ; il fut parmi nous 53 ans, le père de l' orphelin, le soutien du pauvre et de la Veuve ; l' œil d' aveugle, le pied du boiteux, le consolateur des affligés, le bienfaiteur de tous : il vécut 83 ans.

Nos larmes arrosent sa tombe, le ciel comonne ses vertus.

Décédé 18 Juin, 1833.

OBSERVATIONS OF MEDICAL WRITERS UPON THE
NATURE AND EFFECTS OF ANIMAL DECOMPO-
SITION; WITH SOME FACTS, COLLECTED BY THE
AUTHOR IN HIS RESEARCHES UPON THE SUB-
JECT.

Having given very copious extracts from the
works of Dr. Piattoli and others, I subjoin the opinions of more recent enquirers upon the subject of
inhumation in towns, and the dangers resulting
from it. Monsieur Devergie, in his Treatise on
Medical Jurisprudence, (¹) in an article on Judicial
Exhumations, states, that M. Orfila, after having
quoted the various authors mentioned in the preceding pages—who contend that putrid exhalations
from vaults and graves have not only produced
sudden death from asphyxia, but also have frequently
given rise to fatal disease—seems to doubt whether
these dangerous effects were really produced by
such exhalations, or should not be attributed to some
other cause. M. Devergie believes that the deleterious action of putrefying human bodies, can only
be avoided by employing the utmost care during
exhumation. He cites a case in which his friend
M. Piédagnel, who had assisted him in an exhuma-

(¹) Medicine Legale, Vol. 7, p. 316, et seq. Paris, 1836. I
quote M. Devergie as an authority upon this subject; his opinion is
entitled to considerable deference. Mons. D. is Medical Inspector
at the Morgue, in Paris: it is his duty to examine every body
brought there, and to report to the proper authorities the probable
cause of death.

tion for a judicial purpose, was so seriously affected as to be obliged to keep his chamber for six weeks. He was himself also affected from the same cause, *notwithstanding every precaution was taken* to avoid the consequences of exposure to putrefying animal matter.

In reference to the dangers attendant upon exhumation at particular periods, M. Devergie states: first, that the degree will be in proportion to the number of bodies exposed ;—secondly, in regard to the time elapsed since the inhumation ;—and lastly, if in the period of the gaseous putrefaction, and by any cause, a large quantity of gas is suddenly disengaged from a body, asphyxia may be the result. Cases have occurred of grave diggers being suffocated at the moment of opening with a pick-axe the abdomen distended with gas. If the body has been long buried, the surrounding earth is impregnated with a penetrating fœtid odour, which persists for a long time, and, as a considerable period is requisite for digging a grave, individuals who are compelled to breathe such air must suffer more or less from its influence.

Mons. D. states, that the grave diggers who are accustomed to respire these fœtid gases are rarely incommoded, but the person who for the first time attempts such an operation, will certainly experience all its dangerous consequences. M. Devergie then gives an instance of three workmen employed in the removal of the bodies from the Cimetière des Innocens, in Paris, who, neglecting the requisite precautions, nearly paid the penalty with their lives.

M. Orfila states, " that the most the grave diggers experience is a very trivial inconvenience, (¹) even when they have taken no precautions to avoid the effects of putrid exhalations ; that the same may be observed of those medical men who may be obliged to open a body and examine the viscera for some hours. It appears to Mons. O. that this proposition ought only to admit of exception in those cases in which the medical men, (²) or those persons charged with similar duties, are considerably debilitated by previous diseases, and thus their pre-disposition to contract others is increased, or in other cases in which the body being but little ad-advanced in decomposition, and the abdomen con-siderably distended with gas, they may have pierced this cavity mal-adroitly, and thus for a certain time

(¹) M. Orfila has considerably underrated this danger, as I shall prove, from the statements of some grave diggers, whom I have personally interrogated. In the instances I shall adduce, *the young and inexperienced grave diggers have suffered most.*   The old grave digger, too frequently a reckless, abandoned character, is like an old poacher, wise in his own conceit, and not easily taken ; with him " discretion is the better part of valour." Many of these men, however, with all their precaution, are often seriously affected in the execution of their dangerous and disgusting avocation.

(²) A medical man came from Scotland, labouring under con-sumption, and consulted my friend, Dr. James Johnson, and my-self.   The history of his case was this : he made a dissection of the body of a lady who died consumptive, and, being short-sighted, he held his eyes, and, consequently, his mouth, near the lungs, during the examination.   He felt a disagreeable stench, which he could not get rid of ; and that very night a cough arose which

they may be compelled to respire the mephitic gas escaping from the opening."

M. Orfila does not deny that dangerous effects may result from exposure to masses of putrefying bodies ; but he does not admit this danger in a single exhumation. In Paris exhumations are made in considerable numbers, for judicial purposes, (¹) and every precaution is taken.

" The exhumations of the cemetery (²) and of the Eglise des Innocens took place from Dec. 1785 to May 1786, and from Dec. 1786 to Feb. 1787, and from Aug. 1787 to Oct. 1787. *For nearly six years no bodies had been interred* in the cemetery,

never left him from that time till he came to London, and then he was certainly in a state of confirmed consumption.

One solitary case would not be sufficient proof, but I have seen others bearing upon the same point, which incline me to conceive, that the odour of matter in the lungs of an individual who is consumptive, operates either as a specific poison, or as a local irritant, I do not know which, and excites consumption in those who are predisposed to it.—*Armstrong's Practice of Physic, p.* 779.

(¹) The existence of the " Coroner's Court" in England, renders these " judicial exhumations" (with very few exceptions) unnecessary. There are, however, thousands of bodies disinterred annually, in London, for "non-judicial" purposes ; and this is done neither by the sanction of morality, nor by the permission of science.

(²) The ground of the Cimetière des Innocens was first granted by Philippe le Bel, for the burial place of what was then called the " Great Parish :" it was then situated outside of the walls of Paris, and was sufficiently large, the inhabitants being few in number ; but as the population increased, encroachments were gradually made on its confines—it was soon surrounded on all sides by houses, and finally became situated in the centre of Paris. —Memoires pour servir de suite aux Essais Historiques de St. Foix.

no interruption took place in the funeral ceremonies in the church. These operations continued constantly, day and night; each time lasted during a period exceeding ten months. During this long series of operations, a stratum of earth eight or ten feet in thickness, the greater part infected either by the debris of bodies, or by the filth from the neighbouring houses, was taken from the whole surface of the cimetière; and of the church from a surface of four thousand square yards. More than eighty graves were opened and trenched,—forty to fifty of the paupers' graves (fosse communes) were excavated to a depth of eight or ten feet, some quite to the bottom; from eighteen to twenty thousand bodies, belonging to every epoch, were exhumed, with their coffins. This was done in the winter, and also for a very considerable period during times of the greatest heat;—*commenced at first with all possible care, and conducted with every known precaution,*—but continued almost entirely without employing any particular means; no danger appeared during the course of these operations."[1]

It appears then, from the previous extracts, that for six years no burials had taken place in the Cimetière des Innocens; a piece of ground utterly inadequate in size, had been made the receptacle for the dead of a large district for upwards of three centuries; bodies had been placed here, as they are at present in too many of the grounds in London, within a few inches of the surface.

[1] See Devergie's remarks on this statement.—Rappart des Exhumations, par Thouret, p. 10, 1789.

The pauper graves, thirty feet deep and twenty feet square, contained from one thousand to fifteen hundred bodies. When one of these graves was filled, a covering of a foot deep of earth was thrown over it—*each grave remained open about three years*—the time required to fill it. The bodies composing this mass of putrescence, placed in slight and easily destructible coffins, were thus left exposed during this period; thus some of the gaseous products of decomposition would be given off, mixed with, and necessarily diluted by, the atmosphere. Malignant and pestilential diseases were so prevalent in this district, and the popular opinion so strongly expressed, that a decree went forth for the closure of this place. Now it appears to me, that the continued throwing up of portions of earth charged with putrefying animal matter (for the ground in all such places must be constantly offered in fresh surfaces to the atmosphere), would at least have disengaged vast volumes of this gaseous poison, which would be more or less diluted according to many concurring circumstances, as I have before explained.

We have it on record that interments had not been permitted during the six preceding years—the period when the exhumation of the bodies commenced—and thus, as above remarked, the bodies in the super-stratum would have given off some of their products; the result would be found in the various diseases produced,—it should not have been sought for (excepting under peculiar circumstances) in its influence upon the health of the workmen employed, who were men previously well accustomed to the office they undertook. Let it be observed that the two previous exhumations were commenced in the season of the greatest cold, and *terminated*, the first, in *May*—the second, in *February*—the third and concluding one was executed between the months of August and September; thus it will be evident that " the periods of the greatest heat" bore no proportion to the time employed in these operations.

M. Fourcroy, in conjunction with other scientific men, deputed by the French Government to super-intend the health of the workmen employed in these operations, doubtless used " every known precau-tion," and chose *the coldest period of the year for the two first exhumations*,—the principal efforts were made in the months of winter,—the concluding one from August to October, after vast numbers of the bodies had been removed. *Thus the whole surface of the burying ground would, most pro-bably, be exposed by the numerous excavations,* to the surrounding currents of air. During the times of the cessation of the work, a period of many months elapsed.

M. Fourcroy states, that " the grave diggers in-formed him that the putrid process disengages elastic fluid, which inflates the abdomen, and at length bursts it,—that this event instantly causes vertigo, faintness, and nausea, in such persons as unfortunately are within a certain distance of the spot where it happens; when the object of its action is nearer, asphyxia, and death frequently occur. These men regard this period with the utmost terror;—no inducement offered by the philosophers employed in this superintendence, could prevail upon them to assist their researches into this dangerous vapour."

It appears to me extremely improbable that the abdominal cavity is alone concerned in the generation of this fugacious poison,—the products of decomposition must be engendered by the general tissues of the body.(¹) The abdomen may, and possibly does, produce a larger proportion than the other cavities; it may or it may not be more dangerous in its effects. I cannot conceive that the gas generated in the abdomen alone should be capable of distending and even rending asunder, in vaults, the cases in which the body has been deposited, consisting of an inner, a leaden, and always one, frequently two outer ones! This I have repeatedly observed. I wish to advert, in an especial manner to this fact,—it is commonly believed that bodies interred in lead, and deposited in vaults, can exert no injurious influence,—this serious, and indeed highly dangerous error, has crowded the vaults of our churches with dead; by an extension of the same principle, other places, called chapels, have been and continue to be employed as receptacles,—

(¹) This fact may be easily proved by making an incision beneath the skin, some days after death (if the body have been immersed in water), the decomposition and the production of gas will be more rapid; so long as the gas escapes it will inflame.

these have been established in the most densely crowded neighbourhoods, as if in defiance of incontrovertible facts, registered by accurate observers for centuries—facts which prove that the deterioration of that transparent medium—the first and the last food of life—has sent millions of souls prematurely to their last account. Surely it is time to enquire, with how much of wisdom we have admitted the seeds of pestilence in the very midst of us?

Medical men have long noticed the influence of particular agencies on the human constitution, and on the brute species.([1]) Dr. MAJENDIE, seeing that the putrefaction of animal and vegetable matter produced a poison which had the most injurious and fatal effects upon the human body, and which, during the state of decomposition, and under circumstances which produced it in a high state of concentration, was, on a single inhalation, capable of instantaneously causing death; and that, even when diffused in the atmosphere, and spread over a large extent of country, it was the fruitful source of disease and death,—seeing the vast number of facts which had collected, requiring only a single and simple experiment to connect them, demonstrated,

([1]) " From the introduction of the recently dead animal matter the most dangerous consequences arise."—(Macartney on Inflammation.)

M. Orfila and others applied putrid animal matters to wounds in dogs and other quadrupeds, and found that death generally ensued in less than twenty-four hours; extensive local inflammation and constitutional fever were induced.

beyond the possibility of a doubt, that the poison in question was caused by animal and vegetable substances, in a state of putrescency,—by cold and other agents he condensed it, and found that by applying it to an animal, previously in good health, he destroyed life with the most intense symptoms of malignant fever. Ten or twelve drops of water, containing this matter, were injected into the jugular vein of a dog—in a short time it was seized with acute fever—the action of the heart was inordinately excited—the respiration accelerated—the heat of the surface increased—the prostration of strength extreme—the muscular power so exhausted that the animal lay on the ground unable to make the slightest movement; after a period it was seized with the identical black vomit, so characteristic of yellow fever, and what is still more remarkable, is the fact, that by varying the intensity, or the dose of the poison, he could produce fever of almost any type—endowed with almost any degree of mortal power;—when diffused in the atmosphere, this poison taken into the lungs, or absorbed by the larger surface of the skin, enters the blood, and produces diseases of varying malignity, modified as the producing causes be of animal or vegetable origin; thus when the effluvium from marshes, or decayed vegetable matters was employed, intermittent fever (as ague) and remittent fever was produced; but when that from animal matter was experimented with, typhus, and the order of fevers marked by a diminution of power, in all the functions of the body, and a general disposition to putrescency, both in the solids and fluids, invariably followed.

" Now water is not the sole vehicle of miasmatic particles ; the fluid we breathe frequently holds such atoms in suspension ; it is putrid exhalations that give rise to the intermittent fevers of marshy localities, from which the inhabitants sometimes succeed in escaping, by covering the face with a veil during the hours of sleep. The air, while traversing its tissue, is, as it were, sifted, and so reaches the organs of respiration purified of the vegetable or animal molecules with which it is loaded."

" If a small portion of putrid animal matter," says Dr. Armstrong, " be accidentally introduced into the blood in the dissecting room, or if the experiment be made upon the lower animals, it produces a fever, having exactly the characters of typhus, under its continued form. And though, as far as my own observations have gone, malaria or marsh effluvia alone produces typhus fever, under an intermittent, remittent, or continued form ; *yet I believe that putrid matter introduced into the blood, produces an affection so exactly resembling typhus fever* (that, putting out the local affection of the wounded part), *I believe no individual could confidently pronounce that it differed from typhus fever.*"

Dr. Mead, speaking of Grand Cairo, in Egypt, says, " this city is crowded with vast numbers of inhabitants, who. live not only poorly but nastily ; the streets are narrow and close ; the city itself is situated in a sandy plain, at the foot of a mountain, which keeps off the winds which might refresh the air, consequently the heat is rendered extremely stifling; a great canal passes through the midst of the city, which at the overflowing of the Nile is filled with water; on the decrease of the river this canal is gradually dried up, and the people throw into it all manner of filth, carrion, offal, and so on. The stench which arises from this and the mud together is intolerably offensive, and from this source the plague, constantly springing up every year, preys upon the inhabitants, and is stopped only by the return of the Nile, the overflowing of which washes away this load of filth. In Ethiopia, the swarms of locusts are so prodigious, that they sometimes cause a famine by devouring the fruits of the earth, and when they die create a pestilence by the putrefaction of their bodies; this putrefaction is greatly increased by the dampness of the climate, which, during the sultry heats of July and August, is often excessive; the effluvia which arise from this immense quantity of putrefying animal substance, with so much heat and moisture, continually gene-rate the plague in its intensest form, and the Egyptians of old were so sensible how much the putre-faction of dead animals contributed towards breeding the plague, that they worshipped the bird Ibis for the services it did in devouring great numbers of serpents, which they had observed injured by their stench, when dead, as much as by their bite, when alive."

" When the several parts of organized matter have

K

lost that principle which is constantly employed during life, in preserving and keeping them from decay, we find them, when exposed to the atmosphere, soon undergoing a change; their component parts are disunited, new combinations take place, and the properties which formerly characterised them totally vanish.

" These circumstances mark the progress of the putrefactive fermentation, which may be hastened, retarded, or suspended, by the action of other substances, or by the temperature or quality of the air to which they are exposed.

" When putrefaction of the animal organisation commences, the various tissues are confounded, their primary principles are disunited, and new bodies are formed according to the determination of the arrangement between the chemical elective attractions subsisting among these several principles. During life the powers of chemical affinity seem to be suspended, but when animation ceases, chemical union soon begins to exert its influence."

" Among the gases given off during animal decomposition, we must consider sulphuretted hydrogen, the deutoxide of nitrogen, and the chloride of ammonia, as eminently deleterious; for when introduced, in sufficient quantity, into the animal economy, they constantly occasion death; whilst others, such as oxygen, hydrogen, azote, carburetted hydrogen, carbonic acid, carbonic oxide, and the protoxide of azote, only occasion death when introduced into the lungs, because they exclude, by their presence, the only mixture which can support respiration ; in any other point of view they do not occasion death, at least in a rapid manner."—(Bichat. " *Sur la vie et la mort.*")

" The solid parts of the human body are easily resolved into a few elements, either by putrefaction, which they spontaneously undergo by moderate heat, combined with moisture and atmospheric air, or by a heat so great as to destroy the former combination of the elements and produce new ones,—the harder into lime and phosphorus, and the softer into carbon, nitrogen or azote, hydrogen, and oxygen. These elements, variously combined, produce ammonia, carbonic acid, empyreumatic oil, and many fetid vapours, which are not to be detected in the entire animal solid."—(Gregory *Medicina Theoret.*)

" Certain animal fluids act as a species of poison if introduced by means of a wound, or applied upon the more sensible parts of the skin. The substances which operate the most remarkably in this manner, are *animal matters*, in certain stages of decomposition." And again, " the introduction of dead animal matter, by means of a wound, or the application of it to the skin, has often been the cause of a highly dangerous disease, not unfrequently ending in death."

" The two stages of decomposition in the dead body, which render the animal substance most dangerous, are that which takes place *immediately after death,* and *the extreme degree of putrefaction.*" [1]

I adduce the following cases in illustration of the effects produced by the gases generated *during the first periods of putrefaction :*—

[1] Dr. Macartney on inflammation.

In the month of June, in the year 1825, a woman died of typhus fever, in the upper part of the house, No. 17, White Horse Yard, Drury Lane ; the body, which *was buried on the fourth day*, was brought down a narrow staircase : Lewis Swalthey, shoe-maker, then living with his family on the second floor of this house, and now residing at No. 5, Princes Street, Drury Lane, during the time the coffin was placed for a few minutes, in a transverse position, in the door-way of his room, in order that it might pass the more easily into the street, was sensible of a most disgusting odour, which escaped from the coffin. He complained almost immediately afterwards *of a peculiar coppery taste*, which he described as being situated at the base of the tongue and posterior part of the throat ; in a few hours afterwards, he had at irregular intervals slight sensations of chilliness, which before the next sunset had merged into repeated shiverings of considerable intensity ; that evening he was confined to his bed,—he passed through a most severe form of typhus fever ; at the expiration of the third week, he was removed to the fever hospital—he recovered ; he had been in excellent health up to the instant when he was exposed *to this malaria.*

Mr. M——, a patient of mine, some years since was exposed to a similar influence ; a stout muscular man died in his house in the month of June, after a short illness ; on bringing the body down stairs, a disgustingly fetid sanies escaped from the coffin in such considerable quantity, that it flowed down the stairs ; Mr. M. was instantly affected with giddiness, prostration of strength, and extreme lassitude,—he had a peculiar metallic taste in the mouth, which continued some days ; he believes that his health has been deranged from this cause.

I offer the following proofs of the effects of the gases produced by *the extreme degree of putrefaction* :—

My pupil, Mr. J. H. Sutton, accompanied by an individual, for many years occasionally employed in the office of burying the dead, entered the vaults of St. ——— church ; a coffin, "*cruelly bloated,*" as one of the grave diggers expressed it, was chosen for the purpose of obtaining a portion of its gaseous contents. The body, placed upon the top of an immense number of others, had, by the date of the inscription on the plate, been buried upwards of eight years ; the instant the small instrument employed had entered the coffin, a most horribly offensive gas issued forth in large quantities. Mr. S. who unfortunately respired a portion of this vapour, would have fallen but for the support afforded by a pillar in the vault ; he was instantly seized with a suffocating difficulty of breathing (as though he had respired an atmosphere impregnated with sulphur); he had giddiness, extreme trembling, and prostration of strength ; in attempting to leave the vault, he fell from debility ; upon reaching the external air, he had nausea, subsequently vomiting, accompanied with frequent flatulent eructations, highly fetid, and having the same character as the gas inspired. He reached home with difficulty, and was confined to his bed during seven days. The pulse, which was scarcely to be recognised at the wrist,—although the heart beat so tumultuously, that its palpitations might be observed beneath the covering of the bed clothes,—ranged between one hundred and ten and one hundred and twenty-five per minute, during the first three days ; for many days after this exposure, his gait was very vacillating.

The man who accompanied Mr. Sutton was affected in a precisely similar way, and was incapacitated from work for some days ; his symptoms were less in degree—prostration of strength, pains in the head, giddiness, and general involuntary action of the muscles, particularly of the upper limbs, continued for several days afterwards ; these symptoms had been experienced, more or less, by this person, on many previous occasions, but never to so great a degree. I have myself suffered from the same cause, and been compelled to keep my room upwards of a week.

A grave digger was employed to obtain a portion of gas

from a body interred in lead, in the vaults of St. ——— ; the man operated incautiously ; he was struck to the earth, and found lying upon his back ; he was recovered with considerable difficulty.

In a burial ground in Chelsea, within the last seven months, a grave digger was employed in preparing a grave close by a tier of coffins ; he had dug about four feet deep, when the gas issuing from the bodies exposed affected him with asphyxia ; he was found prostrate,—assistance was obtained, and with some difficulty he was recovered.

In the month of August, in the year 1835, a vault was opened in the aisle of the church of Little Birkhampstead, Herts ; the body of a child had been placed in this vault about fifteen months previously ; upon removing the stone, a peculiarly offensive smell was emitted,—the vault was found nearly full of water, in which the coffin was floating. My informant, the then sexton, Benjamin Smith, now living No. 8, Princes Street, Drury Lane, was instantly affected with nausea, followed with diarrhœa, excessive trembling, prostration of strength, and loss of appetite ; these symptoms continued some weeks,— he believes that his health has seriously suffered in consequence. The bricklayer and labourer employed in opening the vault and taking out the water, were also affected, and Mrs. Smith, whilst cleaning the inside of the church, several days afterwards, was sensible of a very offensive odour, which was perceptible during divine service on the Sunday following.

William Jackson, aged 29, a strong, robust man, was employed in digging a grave in the " Savoy ;" he struck his spade into a coffin, from which an extremely disgusting odour arose ; he reached his home, in Clement's Lane, with difficulty ; complained to his wife that he had " had a turn ; the steam which issued from the coffin had made him very ill ;" he had pain in the head, heaviness, extreme debility, lachrymation, violent palpitation of the heart, universal trembling, with vomiting. His wife stated that the cadaverous smell proceeding from his clothes affected her with trembling, and produced head ache; she mentioned that she had been before affected in a similar way, although more slightly, from the same cause. Jackson recovered in a few days, although considerably debilitated; compelled by the poverty of his circumstances, he attempted, seven days afterwards, to dig a grave in Russell Court, Drury Lane; in this ground, long saturated with dead, it was impossible, without disturbing previous occupants, to select a grave; a recently buried coffin was struck into,—the poor fellow was instantly rendered powerless, and dragged out of the grave by John Gray, to whom he was an assistant. Jackson died thirty-six hours afterwards. This case occurred during the visitation of the spasmodic cholera—his death was attributed to that cause. He was buried, I believe, at the expense of the parish; his wife and children are now in Cleveland Street workhouse.

Mr. Paul Graham, residing in my immediate neighbourhood, had buried a child in Russell Court, Drury Lane,—an acquaintance of his was buried in the same ground a few weeks subsequently; the survivors had a suspicion that this body had been exhumed; an undertaker was employed to ascertain the fact. Mr. G. accompanied by another person, was present during the time the lid of the coffin was partially removed; a most offensive effluvium was emitted; he was affected with instant vomiting, head ache, confusion of intellect, prostration of strength, and trembling; the other person became unwell from the same cause; the undertaker had carefully averted his head during the partial removal of the lid of the coffin, and thus escaped its effects. Mr. G. stated to me that no sensation of disgust could have occasioned these symptoms, as the body was not exposed. He has, to this day, a vivid recollection of the offensive odour.

A grave digger was employed, a short time ago, in the ground of St. Clement Danes, Strand; he had excavated a family grave to the depth of sixteen feet, and when the coffin was to have been lowered, he went down by the boards on the sides to the bottom of the grave, and had what is called " a turn ;" he felt as if he had his mouth over brimstone (the taste was " sulphury"); he called out, but was not heard ; he then motioned with his hands, and a rope was lowered down,—he seized hold of the rope, and was pulled up to the surface,—-he was " queer" for a day or two.

In the summer of 1757, five cottagers were digging on the heathy mountain above Eyam, in Derbyshire, which was the place of graves after the church yard became a too narrow repository. These men came to something which had the appearance of having once been linen ; conscious of their situation, they instantly buried it again. In a few days they all sickened of a putrid fever, and three of the five died. The disorder was contagious, and proved fatal to numbers of the inhabitants.

The following important fact was communicated to me by one of the parties immediately concerned :

A Lady died September 7th, 1832, and was buried in the Rector's vault, in St.———'s church, on the 14th. The undertaker had occasion to go down into the vault, near the communion table ; he had done the work of the church nearly thirty years, and was well acquainted with the localities; the grave digger had neglected to take up the slab which covered the vault; the undertaker being pressed for time, with the assistance of the son of the deceased, removed the stone. The two descended, taking with them a light, which was almost instantly extinguished ; upon reaching the lower step of the vault, both were simultaneously seized with sickness, giddiness, trembling, and confusion of intellect ; the undertaker raised his friend, who had fallen on the floor, and with difficulty dragged him out of the vault ; he himself, although a man previously in excellent health, was seized with vomiting the next day, and for twelve months rejected his food : at the end of this period, after having been under the care of many medical men, he consulted Dr. James Johnson, from whom he derived great benefit,—the Doctor pronounced his case to be one of poisoning, from mephitic gases. The patient is convinced that his health has been completely ruined from this cause ; he is now obliged, after a lapse of seven years, " to live entirely by rule." The young gentleman who was with him, was subsequently under the care of many medical men upwards of two years; his principal symptoms, those of a slow poison, developed themselves gradually,—but surely; he was attacked with obstinate ulcerations of the throat, which were not removed until more than two years had elapsed, although he had frequent change of air, and the best medical assistance that could be obtained.

Mr. Tumbleton, a highly respectable undertaker, of No. 4, Warwick Street, Golden Square, informed me that about eleven years ago, he attended the funeral of an " Odd Fellow," on a Sunday, at ENON CHAPEL (particularly mentioned in the sequel); he smelled a disgusting stench ; he was seized, within forty hours, with a violent pain in the back of the left hand, continuing about an hour; he had " cold chills" within half an hour afterwards,—he took a glass of rum and water, and went to bed ; he arose in the morning very ill, and consulted Dr. Burnett, of Golden Square, who ordered him home, and told him that he would " give him three weeks before he got up again." This prognostic was true to a certain extent, for the patient kept his bed nine weeks, with a malignant typhus, and all its concomitant evils.

On the 10th of July last, I was called to attend a widow, named Adams, the house-keeper to a gentleman residing in Gray's Inn Square ; some days before my arrival, she had been attacked with pain, which she referred to the region of the liver. The pulse, on my first visit, was weak and easily compressible, ranging between one hundred and twenty and one hundred and thirty; she complained of no pain—her heart beat tumultuously—the tongue was brown and dry, and protruded with difficulty—her general symptoms were those of action without power. I carefully watched the case; but, notwithstanding all my efforts, my patient sunk on the 22d of the same month. She had been a regular attendant at *Enon chapel.* She died of typhus, accompanied with symptoms of extreme putrescency. Can the cause be problematical?

That I may not unnecessarily multiply cases, I will close this branch of my subject with the evidence given before the Coroner upon the bodies of two men, who lost their lives in a grave, in Aldgate church yard, in September last :—

(Copied from the *Weekly Dispatch* of the 9th Sept. 1838.)

Two Men suffocated in a Grave.

On Friday evening, an inquest was held in the Committee Room of the Workhouse, of the parish of St. Botolph's, Aldgate, on the bodies of Thomas Oakes, the grave digger belonging to Aldgate church, and Edward Luddett, a fish dealer, at Billingsgate market, who came by their deaths on that forenoon under the following circumstances :—Mr. Edward Cheeper, the master of the workhouse, stated, that about eleven o'clock, while passing through Church Passage, Aldgate, he heard the loud screams of a female in the church yard, and he instantly hastened to the spot, and looking into the grave, about twenty feet deep, at the North side of the church yard, he saw the deceased grave digger, Oakes, lying on his back apparently dead. A ladder was instantly procured, and the deceased young man, Luddett, who by this time, with several others, had been attracted to the spot, instantly volunteered to descend to the assistance of Oakes. On his reaching the bottom of the grave, witness called out to him to place the ropes under the arms of Oakes, *and the instant he stooped* to raise the head of Oakes, he appeared as if struck with a cannon ball, and fell back with his head in a different direction to his fellow sufferer, and appeared instantly to expire. King, the former grave digger, made two or three ineffectual attempts to descend, but so foul was the air, that he was obliged to be drawn up again, and it was full twenty-five minutes, or half an hour, before the bodies were taken up by means of a hook attached to a rope. Every possible exertion had been made to recover the bodies, and the conduct of the medical gentleman, Mr. Jones, who promptly attended, was beyond all praise.

Mr. Davis, a member of the Society of Friends, residing in Church Passage, corroborated the last witness, and said he was on the spot, and that every exertion had been used to get up the bodies.

William Mallin deposed, that he and the deceased (Luddett), who was a friend of his, were accidentally passing by the church yard, when they heard that a man was suffocated in a grave, and Luddett volunteered to descend the ladder.

Mrs. Mary Fleetwood stated, that she was the daughter of Philip, the sexton, and her father not being well on that morning, it was the duty of Oakes to ring the chimes at half past ten o'clock, and she finding that he had not done so, went to look for him, and ultimately proceeded to the grave, where she saw him lying at the bottom. She instantly gave an alarm, and Mr. Cheeper and other persons were soon on the spot. The grave was what was termed a deep grave, and had been opened for about four weeks.

Juror (Mr. Heard, a Common Councilman of Holborn.)—Was not this grave what is called a pauper's grave?

Witness.—It was, Sir.—The witness proceeded to state, that such graves as those were kept open until there were seventeen or eighteen bodies interred in them; there was only the body of a still-born infant in the one in question. It was not the custom to put any earth between the coffins in those graves, except in cases where the persons died of contagious diseases, and in that case some slaked lime and a thin layer of earth were put down to separate them. The practice of digging deep graves had been adopted by order of the Churchwardens five or six years ago. Witness knew of instances, *wherein grave diggers could not go down a grave, owing to the foulness of the air;* but she was not aware that the fact had been made known to the Churchwardens. On such occasions, they (the deceased, and his predecessor King) *were in the habit of burning straw, and using other means to dispel the impure air, and then going down. The deceased had been employed as a grave digger about six months,* and was, she should think, about 53 years of age.

William Thomas King, the late grave digger to the parish, made one or two ineffectual attempts to descend, but without being able to succeed.

Mr. Jones, surgeon, of Jewry Street, stated, that a little before eleven o'clock, he proceeded to the church yard, when he found a young man about to descend into the grave. Having at once discovered that the cause of the death of the unfortunate men was carbonic acid gas, generated from decayed animal matter, he would not permit the party to go down, as not the slightest hopes could be entertained of saving the lives of those who were already at the bottom.

The body of the young man was the first taken up, and though he (Mr. Jones) had not the slightest hope of restoring animation, he used every remedy, but of course without effect.

The case of the other man was beyond all hope.

The witness, on being asked his opinion, as to the effect of keeping a grave open a couple of months, replied, that the noxious effluvia from it must be very injurious to health.

Mr. Townley, a respectable tradesman, residing close to the church, complained of the practice adopted in the church yard, which he said was most distressing to the sight, and injurious to the health of the inhabitants of that crowded neighbourhood, and he hoped something would be done about it.

Mr. Tyars, the Deputy of the Ward, said, he had on several occasions sent a presentment, expressing in the strongest language he could use, to the Archdeacon of the diocese, or his Surrogate, descriptive of the filthy state of the vaults and the burying ground, but no notice had been taken of the evil.

He would appeal to the medical gentleman present (Mr. Jones), if burials in a densely populated neighbourhood were not most injurious to health; and for his own part, he hoped the time was not distant when such a practice would be discontinued.

Mr. Jones confirmed the opinion of Mr. Tyars.

The Jury then retired to the inquest room, and the Coroner having summed up the evidence, they returned a verdict of " accidental death" in both cases.

I must now pause—not for want of facts, for they would accumulate, to the fatigue of the reader.— Enough has, I presume, been stated to show the danger of crowded inhumations ; not only to the workmen employed, but also to all persons within the influence of the putrefactive emanations arising from " grave yards."

In the Appendix to the Fourth Report on the Poor Law Commission will be found some important evidence upon the subject of the malarious influences primarily affecting the poor, from which Appendix I extract the following evidence given by Mr. Bullen. Although I dissent from his recommendatory conclusions, I insert his observations as the only direct medical testimony given in the Report relative to the disgusting and highly dangerous condition of the grave yards. Mr. B. has, unfortunately, limited his attention to his own particular district :—

19, Three Tuns Court Road, Redcross Street,
Cripplegate, 8th May, 1838.

GENTLEMEN,

" Seeing from your circulars to the medical officers of the various Unions, that you are desirous of information on the cause of contagion among the working classes, and seeing also that these gentlemen cannot account for the evil, I take the liberty of stating the cause, or at least that which is in a great measure the cause of diffusing the miasma of pestilence among the poor ; how fever among them affects the other classes I leave you to decide.

The subject to which I call your attention, is the cheap burial grounds in the metropolis, which in general are situated in poor neighbourhoods; the graves in these grounds are dug and left open from one Sunday to another, or till they are filled with bodies; no more earth is thrown in them than will just fill up the sides of each coffin; when seven or eight bodies are interred, then it is filled up, and not till then, be that a week or a fortnight; these grounds are in general divided into three or four different prices, as suit the circumstances of the parties; those graves are also dug so close together, that the range of bodies in the adjoining grave may be seen with the heads and feet of others at each end; thus, those long dead, as well as the recent, give forth the mephitical effluvia of death, and it is only for a person that desires to be convinced of the fact, just to visit some of those grounds after a heavy shower of rain; one of the reasons why pestilence attacks the poor first, by their visiting those pest grounds as mourners.

I will now give a case in point: there are four burial grounds for the poor within two hundred yards of each other in that densely populated neighbourhood, Golden Lane, Cripplegate, surrounded with houses, and abutting close to the walls; about this time last year, a court filled with poor people (not forty yards from one of these burial grounds) was attacked by fever; so direful were its effects, that the court was ordered to be closed, unless it was pulled down or thoroughly repaired.

Permit me now to suggest preventives: a strict attention to the burial of the dead, and the burial grounds; absorbents may, and ought to be used, with good effect and at a cheap rate, with interest also to the proprietors at these grounds; absorbents have a tendency to retain and neutralize putrescent matter; inspectors ought to be appointed in every parish to inspect grounds and vaults, and as parish beadles have not so much to do as heretofore, a few pounds to such annually for such extra labour would be the best money paid by any parish; I think that an inspector is quite necessary as one of the preventives, and would be so, with proper instructions. There wants but little observance to prove that the exposed bodies of the dead is the great cause of contagion; next is the decomposed animal and vegetable substances;

a want of ventilation and cleanliness in the houses of the working classes, these all contribute to the worst of maladies; visit many of the houses of the poor, and you will find in thousands of them no ventilation at all, no thorough draught of air, their cellars loaded with rubbish, and their cess-pool seldom emptied. To attend to these also is a most essential part of the duty of those who desire to see the metropolis healthy.

I remain, &c.

(Signed) ROBERT BULLEN.

To the Honourable the Poor Law Commissioners,
Somerset House.

From the same Report I extract the following :—
To the Poor Law Commissioners.

SIRS, 1st May, 1838.

The Poor Law Commissioners have been rightly informed that a *very malignant typhus fever has prevailed here for some time past, and indeed rages now as bad as ever, and, I think, more fatal in its course. In looking* over my books I find that, in the space *of nine months, I have attended upwards of* 500 *pauper cases ; but I cannot trace the disease to any local cause, for we have in the parish of St. George very good drainage through the parish, and very little accumulated filth,* with the exception of Falcon Court, White Street, Noel's Court, Hunter Street, and Peter Street (Mint); *but here the disease does not exist more severe than over the parish in general.*

The principal causes by which it continues and is propagated, I think, are, First,—Intemperate habits of the poor ; indulging in spirituous liquors, with little solid food; their irregularity of being at home. Second,—Want of cleanliness, both in person and habitation ; wearing the same clothes ; sleeping together at the time when the fever rages in the house or room. Third,—Want of ventilation; often their rooms are seldom swept, washed, or ventilated, for months together ; I frequently attend three or four in the same room, generally taking the disease in succession.

Typhus fever has been so contagious that my two assistants caught it in a severe form, but ultimately recovered.

In consequence of all the hospitals being full, and our workhouse not completed, the severity of the disease is more felt, for I cannot get the first case removed to prevent others suffering from the first cause; therefore, will the Poor Law Commissioners allow me, most respectfully, to suggest to them the propriety of urging the completion of the workhouse, as in that case great part of the evil which now exists would be removed, as I could appropriate a room or two for the reception of urgent cases, and would lessen the burthen of the rate payers, for most of the distress now in existence arises from want of accommodation in the workhouse.

I remain, &c.

(Signed)   EDWARD EVANS, Surgeon, &c.
63, Blackman Street, Borough.

I cannot help expressing my surprise that Dr. Southwood Smith, whose name and reputation in all matters connected with science and literature are so well established, and who appears to have been professionally consulted by the Poor Law Commissioners, and to have taken a prominent part in the enquiry into the causes affecting the health of the metropolis, should not have given his attention more especially to the condition of the grave yards in the districts which he personally examined, and which, in many other respects, he has so ably and so accurately described.   The omission to scrutinize the "receptacles of the dead" will appear even more extraordinary, since from the following extract it is evident that the Doctor has been very observant of the dangerous consequences resulting from putrefactive exhalations:—

"It is known to every one, that the putrefaction of vegetable and animal matter produces a poison, which is capable of exerting an injurious action on the human body. But the extent to which this poison is generated, the conditions favourable to its production, and the range of its noxious agency, are not sufficiently understood and appreciated.

" It is a matter of experience that, during the decomposition of dead organic substances, whether vegetable or animal, aided by heat and moisture, and other peculiarities of climate, a poison is generated, which, when in a state of high concentration, is capable of producing instantaneous death, by a single inspiration of the air in which it is diffused.

" Experience also shows that this poison, even when it is largely diluted by admixture with atmospheric air, and when, consequently, it is unable to prove thus suddenly fatal, is still the fruitful source of sickness and mortality, partly in proportion to its intensity, and partly in proportion to the length of time and the constancy with which the body remains exposed to it.

" The exhalations which accumulate in close, ill-ventilated, and crowded apartments, in the confined situations of densely populated cities, where no attention is paid to the removal of putrefying and excrementitious substances, consist chiefly of animal matter; such exhalations contain a poison which produces continued fever of the typhoid character. There are situations, as has been stated, in which the poison generated is so intense and deadly, that a single inspiration of it is capable of producing in-

L

stantaneous death ; there are others in which a few inspirations of it are capable of destroying life in from two to twelve hours ; and there are others, again, in which the poison generated, although not so immediately fatal, is still too potent to be breathed long, even by the most healthy and robust, without producing fever of a highly dangerous and mortal character.

" But it would be a most inadequate view of the pernicious agency of this poison, if it were restricted to the diseases commonly produced by its direct operation. It is a matter of constant observation, that even when not present in sufficient intensity to produce fever, by disturbing the function of some organ, or set of organs, and thereby weakening the general system, this poison acts as a powerful predisposing cause of some of the most common and fatal maladies to which the human body is subject." —*(Dr. Smith's Report to the Poor Law Commissioners, May,* 1838.)

DESCRIPTION AND STATE OF SOME OF THE METROPOLITAN BURYING PLACES.

The customs of different nations respecting interment show that in every country danger was apprehended from the proximity of the dead to the living. Experience justified the apprehension; and the French Government, as before stated, stands preeminent in its arrangements to secure the health, and, consequently, the happiness of its members. The dead interred within their cities have been removed; public cemeteries (¹) have been established at a distance from towns; sanatory laws have been enacted and rigidly enforced. New York, Pennsylvania, and a few other States have followed the example; but England yet retains within the bosom of her population the germs, the nuclei of diseases, the food, if not the principles, of malignant epidemics. To what cause is this supineness on the part of the British Government to be attributed?

It has been shown that pestilential diseases and

(¹) Although in no way connected, directly or indirectly, with any of the private speculations of the day in this country, inviting the attention of the public to cemeteries out of the precincts of populous neighbourhoods, I most sincerely wish the efforts of the projectors may prove successful; but, aware of the uncertainty, and even danger, of private speculations on so important a subject, I am anxious to see the cares of the Government earnestly engaged in providing suitable public depositories for the dead, and in securing, by judicious and efficient regulations, the exclusive employment of the places so chosen, for the purposes of interment; prohibiting all private dwellings from proximity to those districts.

the loss of human life have resulted from the poisonous exhalations of the church yard in other countries, and I have already shown, that, from similar causes, effects equally destructive have been experienced in our own country. Indeed the burying grounds of the metropolis, in particular, are so overcharged with dead, and even saturated with the products of putrefaction, that our comparative freedom from pestilence can only be ascribed to the natural or acquired power of resistance of its inhabitants, to favourable seasons, or to diminished temperature.

From the opinions previously quoted, upon the nature and effects of the putrefactive process, in animal and vegetable substances, it appears "*that the effluvium from marshes and decaying vegetable matter produces* INTERMITTENT AND REMITTENT FEVERS; and *that the exhalations from animal putrescency are productive of* TYPHUS FEVER, *and fevers marked by a diminution of power in all the functions of the body, and a general disposition to putrescency both in the solids and fluids.*"

I had been frequently called to cases of typhus fever in an aggravated form in my immediate neighbourhood, I consequently endeavoured to ascertain the causes more immediately in operation; and, although willing to admit that the neighbourhood of slaughter houses—the decomposition of vegetable substances—the narrowness of the streets, and the filth and poverty of some of the inhabitants, greatly contributed to the furtherance of the mischief, I felt convinced that the grand cause of all the evil was the immediate proximity of the burial places, public as well as private.

From the following descriptions, the reader will be able to form a just estimate of the dangers by which he is surrounded :—

CLEMENT'S LANE.—This is a narrow thoroughfare on the eastern side of Clare Market; it extends from Clare Market to the Strand, and is surrounded by places, from which are continually given off emanations from animal putrescence. The back windows of the houses on the east side of the lane look into a burying ground called the " Green Ground," in Portugal Street, presently to be described; on the west side the windows (if open) permit the odour of another burying place—a private one, called Enon Chapel—to perflate the houses; at the bottom—the south end—of this Lane, is another burying place, belonging to the Alms Houses, (¹) within a few feet of the Strand, and in the centre of the Strand are the burying ground and vaults of St. Clement Danes ; in addition to which, there are several slaughter houses in the immediate neighbourhood : so that in a distance of about two hundred yards, in a direct line there are four burying grounds ; and the living here breathe on all sides an atmosphere impregnated with the odour of the dead. The inhabitants

(¹) This place is, I believe, filled with dead ; many of the coffins being near the surface.

of this narrow thoroughfare are very unhealthy; nearly every room in every house is occupied by a separate family. Typhus fever in its aggravated form has attacked by far the majority of the residents, and death has made among them the most destructive ravages.

BURYING GROUND, PORTUGAL STREET.—This ground belongs to the parish of St. Clement Danes; it is commonly known by the name of the " Green Ground," and has been in use as a burying place beyond the memory of man.

The soil of this ground is saturated, absolutely saturated, with human putrescense. On Saturday the 27th April, 1839, at 5, P.M. I went, accompanied by a friend, to Nos. 30 and 31, Clement's Lane, and, upon looking through the windows of the back attics, we saw two graves open, close to the south-eastern extremity of this burying ground. Several bones were lying on the surface of the grave nearest to us—a large heap of coffin wood was placed in readiness for removal, and, at a small distance, a heap covered with coarse sacking, was observed, which, when the covering was taken off, proved also to be long pieces of coffin wood, evidently not in a decayed state. The nails were very conspicuous. Several basketfuls of this wood were taken to a building at the south-west extremity of the ground. We were informed that this sight was by no means a novel one; it was commonly—almost daily, observed. The cloth covering of the wood appeared to be nearly as fresh as when interred. The grave diggers were seen to take off tin plates from the coffins broken up. This desecration of the grave has not escaped the notice of the passer-by, as is proved from the following letter to the editor of the *Times* newspaper, which was published on the 25th of June last:—

SIR,

Passing along Portugal Street on Saturday evening, about ten minutes before seven, I was much shocked at seeing two men employed in carrying baskets (¹) of human bones from the corner of the ground next the old watch-house (where there was a tarpaulin hung over the rails to prevent their being seen, and where they appeared to be heaped up in a mound), to the back of the ground through a small gate.

Where this leads to I do not know; but I should be glad, through the medium of your invaluable journal to ask, why is this desecration ?

Sir,—I feel more particularly than many might do, as I have seen *twelve* of my nearest and dearest relatives consigned to the grave in that ground; and I felt that, perhaps, I might at the moment be viewing, in the basket of skulls which passed before me, those of my own family thus brutally exhumed.

At all events, for the sake of the community at large, it should be inquired into.

J. M.

The complaint here made is, unfortunately applicable to most of the metropolitan burying grounds, under the present system; a system as dangerous

---

(¹) Many waggon loads were removed to a receptacle situated on the north east of this ground; some idea may be formed of the quantity, when I state that five men were employed about a week in their removal.

as it is revolting and disgusting : the evil can only be effectually destroyed by an enactment of the Legislature, prohibiting altogether interment within cities, towns, or densely populated villages.

The effluvia from this ground, at certain periods, are so offensive, that persons living in the back of Clement's Lane are compelled to keep their windows closed ; the walls even of the ground which adjoins the yards of those houses, are frequently seen reeking with fluid, which diffuses a most offensive smell. Who can wonder, then, that fever is here so prevalent and so triumphant?

In the beginning of the present year, I was called upon to attend a poor man, who lived at 33, Clement's Lane ; his health was broken, his spirits depressed, and he was fast merging into that low form of fever of which this locality has furnished so many examples. I found him in the back room of an extremely dirty house, his wife and family with him. On looking into the " Green Ground," through the window of his room, I noticed a grave open within a few feet of the house ; the sick man replied to my observations, " Ah, that grave is just made for a poor fellow who died in this house, in the room above me ; *he* died of typhus fever, from which his wife has just recovered,—*they have kept him twelve days*, and now they are going to put him under my nose, by way of warning to me."

About twenty years since, it was the custom in the " Green Ground" to bury the poor in a vault underneath the pauper's promenade, which is now flagged over—trap doors covered the entrance to the vault; a large chimney or shaft, rising from about the centre of the vault, carried off the products of decomposition from this place; the smell, I am informed by a respectable man, was disgustingly offensive, and was frequently intolerable during hot weather. The bodies were buried in slight deal three-quarter stuff coffins; these were soon destroyed: they were packed, as is the custom, one upon the other; the superincumbent weight, aided by the putrefactive process, had deranged several of the bodies; in replacing one of the coffins, three guineas fell from it; it was supposed that the money had been clutched in the hand previous to death; a more rational supposition is, that the nurse had hidden the money in the coffin, but that the opportunity had not offered of removing it.

The workhouse, at the north-eastern extremity of this ground, has, within the last few weeks, been disused; and the building, it appears, is about to be converted into an hospital, for the reception of patients, belonging to the Medical and Surgical department of King's College: from the high standing of the gentlemen connected with this establishment, I can entertain no doubt that the condition of the earth's surface, and, consequently, the salubrity of the surrounding atmosphere, will be primary objects of attention before patients are admitted.

In the middle of the north-east boundary of this

burying ground is placed a grave-stone with the following inscription :—

HERE LYE THE REMAINS OF
HONEST JO MILLER,
WHO WAS
A TENDER HUSBAND,
A SINCERE FRIEND,
A FACETIOUS COMPANION,
AND AN EXCELLENT COMEDIAN ;
HE DEPARTED THIS LIFE THE 15TH DAY OF
AUGUST, 1738, AGED 54 YEARS.

If humour, wit, and honesty could save
The hum'rous, witty, honest, from the grave,
The grave had not so soon this tenant found,
Whom honesty, and wit, and humour crown'd :
Could but esteem and love preserve our breath,
And guard us longer from the stroke of death,
The stroke of death on him had later fell,
Whom all mankind esteem'd and lov'd so well.

S. DUCK.

FROM RESPECT TO SOCIAL WORTH,
MIRTHFUL QUALITIES, AND HISTRIONIC EXCELLENCE,
COMMEMORATED BY POETIC TALENT IN HUMBLE LIFE,
THE ABOVE INSCRIPTION, WHICH TIME
HAD NEARLY OBLITERATED, HAS BEEN PRESERVED
AND TRANSFERRED TO THIS STONE BY ORDER OF
MR. JAMES BUCK, CHURCHWARDEN,
A.D. 1816.

ENON CHAPEL.—This building is situated about midway on the western side of Clement's Lane ; it is surrounded on all sides by houses, crowded by inhabitants, principally of the poorer class. The upper part of this building was opened for the purposes of public worship about 1823; it is separated from the lower part by a boarded floor : this is used as a burying place, and is crowded at one end, even to the top of the ceiling, with dead. It is entered from the inside of the chapel by a trap door; the rafters supporting the floor are not even covered with the usual defence—lath and plaster. Vast numbers of bodies ([1]) have been placed here in pits, dug for the purpose, the uppermost of which were covered only by a few inches of earth ; a sewer runs angularly across this " burying place." A few years ago, the Commissioners of Sewers, for some cause, interfered,—and ultimately another arch was thrown over the old one; in this operation many bodies were disturbed and mutilated. Soon after interments were made, a peculiarly long narrow black fly was observed to crawl out of many of the coffins ; this insect, a product of the putrefaction of the bodies, was observed on the following season to be succeeded by another, which had the appearance of a common bug ([2]) with wings. The children attending the SUNDAY SCHOOL, held in *this chapel*, in which these insects were to be seen crawling and flying, in vast numbers, during the summer months, called them " body bugs,"—the stench was fre-

([1]) From the most authentic information, I have reason to believe, that since the establishment of this place, from ten to twelve thousand bodies have been deposited here, not one of which has been placed in lead.

([2]) I have not been able to obtain a scientific description of these insects.

quently intolerable; one of my informants states, that he had a peculiar taste in his mouth during the time of worship, and that his handkerchief was so offensive, that immediately upon his return home, his wife used to place it in water. The parish authorities interfered upon the subject of poor rates, proposing to impose a mere nominal one, if the place were closed; this was done for about twelve months. In defiance of opinion, however, it was again employed for the purposes of interment, and has been so used up to the present time. I am acquainted with many who have been seriously affected by exhalations from the vault, and who have left the place in consequence.

Some months since, hand bills were circulated in the neighbourhood, "*requesting parents and others to send the children of the district to the Sunday School,*" *held immediately over the masses of putrefaction in the vault beneath.*

Residents about this spot, in warm and damp weather, have been much annoyed with a peculiarly disgusting smell; and occasionally, when the fire was lighted in a house abutting upon this building, an intolerable stench arose, which it was believed did not proceed from a drain. Vast numbers of rats infest the houses; and meat exposed to this atmosphere, after a few hours, becomes putrid.

This place is familiarly known among undertakers by the appellation of the " Dust Hole," and is a specimen of one of the evils which sprang up during the operation of certain laws that were hostile to the cultivation of anatomical science, which have happily now been repealed. The professed security of the dead was made the pretext; individual advantage was the real object for depositories of this description. The health and comforts of the living were entirely disregarded, and the annoyance and dangers, resulting from the proximity and effluvia of decaying animal substances were submitted to, and hazarded by survivors, rather than subject themselves to the tormenting anxieties which arise from the apprehensions of a brutal exhumation.

I have several times visited this Golgotha. I was struck with the total disregard of decency exhibited,—numbers of coffins were piled in confusion —large quantities of bones were mixed with the earth, and lying upon the floor of this cellar (for vault it ought not to be called), lids of *coffins* might be trodden upon at almost every step.

My reflections upon leaving the masses of corruption here exposed, were painful in the extreme; I want language to express the intense feelings of pity, contempt, and abhorrence I experienced. Can it be, thought I, that in the nineteenth century, in the very centre of the most magnificent city of the universe, such sad, very sad mementos of ignorance, cupidity, and degraded morality, still exist? Possibly I am now treading over the mouldering remains of many, once the cherished idols of the heart's best and purest affections,—here, thought I, may repose onewho has had his cares, his anxieties—

who, perchance, may have well fulfilled life's duties, and who has tasted its pleasures and its sorrows,—here he sleeps as I must sleep; yet I could not but desire that I might have a better resting place—a *Christian* burial.

St. Clement's Church, *Strand.*—There is a vault under this church called the " *Rector's Vault,*" the descent into which is in the aisle of the church near the communion table, and when opened the products of the decomposition of animal matter are so powerful, that lighted candles, passed through the opening into the vault, are instantly extinguished; the men at different times employed, have not dared to descend into the vault until two or three days had elapsed after it had been opened, during which period the windows of the church also were opened to admit the perflation of air from the street to occupy the place of the gas emitted;—thus a diluted poison is given in exchange from the dead to the living in one of the most frequented thoroughfares of the metropolis. The other vaults underneath the church are also much crowded with dead. From some cause, at present doubtful, these vaults were discovered to be on fire [1] upwards of fifty years ago; they continued burning for some days, and many bodies were destroyed.

At the eastern side of this church a pump was for-

[1] This is not a very unusual circumstance; the vaults underneath St. James's Church, Jermyn Street, many years since, were on fire.

merly fixed; this, within the previous month, has been removed, and a brick erection placed upon its site; the well was sunk in the year 1807, but the water had become so offensive, both to smell and taste, that it could not be used by the inhabitants, owing, most probably, to the infiltration of the dissolved products of human putrefaction. (1) Graves certainly

(1) M. LAVOISIER, in the *Histoire de l'Academie des Sciences* for 1786, has shewn that water is decomposed by animal and vegetable substances. He proves that this decomposition takes place in the several processes to which animal and vegetable substances are subjected, and he adds, that the observations which he has made on vegetable substances will apply to animal matters; these, he observes, are equally the result of a triple combination of oxygen, hydrogen, and carbon; they contain neither the water, the carbonic acid, nor the oil already formed, but their elements or component parts are contained in them. These phenomena are, he observes, still more complicated, since they possess a fourth principle—azote—which, combining with the hydrogen, forms the ammonia or volatile alkali. He further states, that the observations made by M. Fourcroy, on the conversion of the muscular parts into a fatty matter, after the lapse of a very considerable time in the cimetiéres, also support this theory; the oxygen, he observes, has been abstracted by some circumstance, allowing the hydrogen and carbon only to remain, which are the materials that compose the fatty matter.

Dr. Reid mentions an important fact, illustrating the cause of putro-adynamic fevers,—a cause which exists to a greater extent than is supposed, especially in large cities, although in a much less degree than in the instance about to be adduced. At Valladolid, during the war in Spain, the palace of the " Holy Inquisition" was appointed for the barracks of a British regiment. Under the colonnade was a well, from which water could be drawn into the uppermost stories. This water had a sweetish decayed taste; but, for the want of better, the soldiers used it both for drinking and

have been dug very near to this well, and the land springs have risen to within a few feet of the surface.

From information recently obtained, it appears that several persons have been buried near this spot, and that in particular, the coffins of two very respectable inhabitants of the parish, as soon as let down into the graves, sunk below the surface of the water which had percolated into them; it is even stated that the deceased, from a wish to be buried in a watery grave, and knowing the situation, had particularly fixed upon it for the interment of their bodies.

Can it be surprising, then, that the water of this well should have become impregnated and corrupted?

The following anecdote is amusing and instructive :—

A correspondent in the Farmer's Magazine, for May, 1839, says, " To show the great power of cattle in discovering nauseous smells, the writer of this article cannot avoid mentioning a curious circumstance that was a short time since related to him by a gentleman of undoubted veracity. A cow, belonging to the above gentleman, was found dead in a ditch of the pasture, and was

cooking. No other regiment in the garrison was so unhealthy; *and the prevailing disease was putrid fever, of which there was not the slightest symptom in any of the other regiments.* At last the reason was discovered: skeletons were found in the well, and several were observed with pieces of the flesh adhering to the bones. If the chlorides of soda or of lime had been then known, or if that which had been long previously recommended had been employed, the mortality from this fever, and from putro-adynamic dysentery, would not have been so great as it proved during the Peninsular campaigns.—Copeland's Dict. Prac. Med.

deeply buried there : about two years after this, a trough was fixed in the field near to this spot, and supplied by a small run of water ; the cattle refused to drink, or even to come near the water. On seeing this the gentleman made his men dig about the place, to see if there was anything particular in the soil, when they discovered the dry bones of the animal that had two years previously been buried there. The bones were removed, two or three cart loads of the soil carried away, and replaced by fresh. After this the cattle drank freely. Had the supply of water passed over the remains of the dead animal, we could easily imagine the cause of this aversion ; but this was not the case, as the water came in an open gutter, above the trough, and the animal was buried below the trough, and lower down the hill."

St. Martin in the Fields.—The old burying ground adjoining the church has been broken up for the purpose of making improvements in the city of Westminster ; the dead were disinterred, and their remains removed to vaults, called catacombs. This circumstance is commemorated by the following inscription, on the north side of St. Martin's church :—

" These catacombs were constructed at the expense of the Commissioners of his Majesty's Woods and Forests, in exchange for part of the burial ground of this parish, on the south side of the church, given up for the public improvements, and were consecrated by the Lord Bishop of London on the 7th day of June, 1831. The Rev. Geo. Richards, D.D. Vicar ; John Smith, James Aldridge, Church - wardens."

The description of the new vaults is taken from the *Sunday Times* of June 12th, 1831 :—

" The new vaults under St. Martin's burying ground are the most capacious structure of the sort in London. They were opened on Tuesday, at the consecration of the new burial ground.

M

They consist of a series of vaults, running out of one another in various directions; they are lofty, and when lighted up, as on Tuesday, really presented something of a comfortable appearance. Some of the vaults having been quite filled with the coffins taken out of the old burying grounds, have been blocked up at both ends,—in fact, hermetically sealed, a plan which is to be adopted with the other vaults in succession, when the cold tenants shall be sufficiently numerous. They are of tolerable height; about ten feet to the turn of the arch, twenty in width, and nearly forty in length; capable of holding, we should suppose, one thousand coffins each. They are white-washed around, and at top, and the flagging at the bottom keeps them dry beneath the foot. All the leaden coffins, removed from the burial ground, are placed in one vault. On the end of one conspicuously placed beneath a grating, through which the light descends, was inscribed the name of Lady Hannah Gordon. There are arcades or corridors leading to the vaults, which branch off right and left, along which are ranges of head-stones, recording the names of individuals whose bones, removed from their old resting place, repose beneath. These have a handsome appearance, lying as they do, at either side, close to the wall, and looking somewhat like an artificial balustrade, flanking the wall in the centre. Crowds of ladies perambulated the vaults for some time, and the whole had more the appearance of a fashionable promenade than a grim repository of decomposing mortality."

DRURY LANE BURYING GROUND belongs to the parish of St. Martin's in the Fields;—many thousands of bodies have been here deposited. The substratum was, some years since, so saturated with dead, that the place " was shut up" for a period. The ground was subsequently raised to its present height—*level with the first floor windows surrounding the place,* and in this superstratum vast numbers of bodies have, up to this period, been deposited. A short time since a pit was dug (a very common practice here) in one corner of the ground; in it many bodies were deposited at different periods, the top of the pit being covered only with boards. This ground is a most intolerable and highly dangerous nuisance to the entire neighbourhood. Rather more than two years ago, in making three areas to the centre houses on the western side of this burying ground, many bodies were disturbed and mutilated; the inhabitants of the houses are frequently annoyed by the most disgusting and repulsive sights.

RUSSELL COURT, DRURY LANE.—This BURYING GROUND belongs to the parish of *St. Mary le Strand*; in its original state it was below the level of the adjoining ground,—now, the surface is on a line with the first floor windows, of the houses entirely surrounding this place. It has long been in a very disgusting condition, but within the last month the surface has been " cleaned up," and the whole may now be called "the whited sepulchre." A man who had committed suicide was buried here on the 20th May, 1832; the body was in the most offensive condition, and was placed within a very little distance of the surface.

About twenty years ago, Mr. ———, a very respectable tradesman in the neighbourhood, was employed to make a " cold air drain" at the west end of this ground; for this purpose it was necessary to cut through the wall of an adjoining house; on taking up the ground floor of this house, large quantities of human bones were found scattered about,—it was supposed they had been dragged thither by rats, vast numbers of which annoy the inhabitants in the proximity of this burying ground.

ST. PAUL'S, COVENT GARDEN.—The burying ground adjoining the church, with difficulty admits an increase. On a recent occasion, the grave digger had to make several trials before he could find room for a new tenant, and he assured me that on several occasions, he had been driven from the attempt of digging a grave, and compelled to throw back the earth, owing to the dangerous effluvia he experienced from the soil. The vault underneath the church is also crowded.

ST. GILES'S BURYING GROUND.—St. Giles's parish has the melancholy notoriety of originating the plague in 1665.(¹) It was the fashion in those days to ascribe that visitation to *imported contagion.* I will not pause to enquire whether in the disgusting condition of many portions of this and other districts sufficient causes may not be operating to produce an indigenous effect, which might again be ascribed to a foreign origin.

Pennant, in his account of London, p. 157, expresses himself strongly on the condition of this

(¹) " The year 1665 became memorable in London by the dreadful ravages of the GREAT PLAGUE, which first broke out at a house in Long Acre, near Drury Lane, in the parish of St. Giles in the Fields."—*(London and Middlesex, by E. W. Brayley.)*

church yard :—" I have," says he, " in the church yard of St. Giles's, seen with horror, a great square pit, with many rows of coffins piled one upon the other, all exposed to sight and smell; some of the piles were incomplete, expecting the mortality of the night. I turned away disgusted at the view, and scandalized at the want of police, which so little regards the health of the living, as to permit so many putrid corpses, tacked between some slight boards, *dispersing their dangerous effluvia over the capital,* to remain unburied. Notwithstanding a compliment paid to me in one of the public papers, of my having occasioned the abolition of the horrible practice, it still remains uncorrected in this great parish. The reform ought to have begun in the place just stigmatised."

That the present condition of this burying place is not much improved, will be seen by the following extract, taken from the *Weekly Dispatch* of September 30th, 1838:—

" ST. GILES'S CHURCH YARD.—What a horrid place is Saint Giles's church yard! It is full of coffins, up to the surface. Coffins are broken up before they are decayed, and bodies are removed to the " bone house" before they are sufficiently decayed to make their removal decent. The effect upon the atmosphere, in that very densely populated spot, must be very injurious. I had occasion to attend the church with several gentlemen, on Tuesday; being required to wait, we went into this Golgotha; near the east side we saw a finished grave, into which had projected a nearly sound coffin; half of the coffin had been chopped away to complete the shape of the new grave. A man was standing by with a barrowful of sound wood, and several bright coffin plates. I asked him " Why is all this?" and his answer was, " O, it is all Irish "

We then crossed to the opposite corner, and there is the " bone house," which is a large round pit; into this had been shot, from a wheelbarrow, the but partly-decayed inmates of the smashed coffins. Here, in this place of " Christian burial," you may see human heads, covered with hair; and here, in this " consecrated ground," are human bones with flesh still adhering to them. On the north side, a man was digging a grave; he was quite drunk, so indeed were all the grave diggers we saw. We looked into this grave, but the stench was abominable. We remained, however, long enough to see that a child's coffin, which had stopped the man's progress, had been cut, longitudinally, right in half; and there lay the child, which had been buried in it, wrapped in its shroud, resting upon the part of the coffin which remained. The shroud was but little decayed. I make no comments ; every person must see the ill effects if such practices are allowed to continue.".

The vaults of this church are crowded with dead ; they are better ventilated than many others,—so much the worse for the public.

I have been the more particular in the foregoing statements, as the places described are situated in my immediate neighbourhood, and first attracted my especial attention to the fatal consequences that must ultimately arise, if the practice of interment in the midst of the living be not speedily abolished altogether, or at least confined within the narrowest limits. The following brief outline of the state of several other churches and grounds of the metropolis will prove, that the evils apprehended are confined to no particular locality; but that, wherever the enquiry is instituted, similar facts are established, and dangers and results equally fatal, and injurious to the health of the inhabitants, may, with too much reason, be apprehended.

ALDGATE CHURCH YARD.—The state of this burying ground is truly alarming. The fatal occurrence which took place in September, 1838, during the opening of a grave (the particulars of which will be found at p. 138), not only excited considerable alarm at the moment, but must convince the most sceptical, of the dangers of inhumation in the church yards of the metropolis. This ground is crowded to excess.

The inscription on a tomb-stone in front of the High Street, is worth preserving :—

" Sacred to the memory of Thomas Ebrall, Citizen and Corn Meter, who was shot by a Life Guardsman, on the 9th April, 1810, in the shop of Mr. Goodire, Fenchurch Street, and died on the 17th of the same month, in the 24th year of his age.

The Coroner's Inquest brought in a verdict, Murdered by a Life Guardsman, unknown.

" Thus saith the Lord God, my right hand shall not spare the sinners, and my sword shall not cease over them that shed innocent blood upon the earth."—*Second Esdras, c. 15, v. 21, 22.*

———

Also of Thomas Ebrall, who, worn out with grief for the loss of the above dutiful Son, departed this life August 23d, 1810, aged 48 years.

WHITECHAPEL CHURCH.—The VAULTS *underneath this church,* have been suffered to fall into a very dilapidated state ; the smell from them, owing to the exposed and decayed state of some of the coffins is very offensive.

The BURIAL GROUND, *adjoining the church,*

abuts upon one of the greatest thoroughfares in London, and is placed in the centre of a densely populated neighbourhood; its appearance altogether is extremely disgusting, and I have no doubt whatever, that the putrefactive process which is here very rapidly going on, must, in a great measure, be the cause of producing, certainly of increasing, the numerous diseases by which the lower order of the inhabitants of this parish have so frequently been visited. The ground is so densely crowded as to present one entire mass of human bones and putrefaction. These remains of what once were gay, perhaps virtuous and eminent, are treated with ruthless indifference. They are exhumed by shovelfuls, and disgustingly exposed to the pensive observations of the passer-by—to the jeers or contempt of the profane or brutal. It appears almost impossible to dig a grave in this ground without coming into contact with some recent interment, and the grave digger's pick is often forced through the lid of a coffin when least expected, from which so dreadful an effluvium is emitted, as to occasion immediate annoyance; most of the graves are very shallow,—some entire coffins, indeed, are to be found within a foot and a half of the surface.

In digging a foundation for a new wall, on the eastern side of the church, the workmen penetrated through a mass of human bones eight or ten feet in thickness; these bones were thrown out, and for some time lay exposed to public view, scattered over the ground in a loathsome humid state; two or three pits were afterwards dug to the depth of eight or ten feet, as common repositories for these bones; and the pits were filled up to within a few inches of the top, with a slight covering of earth over them; family graves also were disturbed, and many coffins exposed,—some of them literally cut in two; in consequence of which much altercation arose between the churchwardens and parishioners. Coffin wood is plentifully strewed over the ground in a rotten and decomposed state. There is a mural monument in the church yard, to the memory of four " twin" children, born in the year 1813. Funerals frequently take place, and much sickness has latterly prevailed in the neighbourhood, especially among children.

The *poor ground*, a little distance from the church, is as thickly crowded with the remains of the dead as the burying ground adjoining to the church.

St. Mary's Catholic Chapel, *Moor Fields.*— The burial ground adjoining this chapel is crowded to excess, and has been closed for several years past. The vaults under the chapel are principally for private persons; none but the more wealthy Catholics are interred in them.

There is a burial ground belonging to this chapel in Poplar, where a great many of the poor Irish are interred; this place too is very full; the ground is very damp, and cannot be dug beyond five or six feet " without coming to water;" many of the bodies lie near the surface, slightly covered over with earth ; the neighbourhood is thickly inhabited, much sickness latterly prevailed, both among children and adults.

Another burial ground belonging to this chapel, in Dog Row, Whitechapel Road, is also excessively full, and requires to be dug with the greatest care.

SPITAL FIELDS GROUND adjoins the church, and is literally overcharged with dead. The vault underneath the body of the church is also very much crowded.

BETHNAL GREEN.—There are two burial grounds in this parish, called the *old* and *new ground*; the *old ground*, like that of Whitechapel, is very full,— from eight to ten funerals have taken place daily, and three or four grave diggers are constantly employed. The depth of the graves is, on an average, little more than four feet,—at a greater depth the water flows in. The *new ground* is situated in the Bethnal Green Road, adjoining to the new church.

STEPNEY.—The burial ground adjoins the church, and is crowded to excess; footpaths cross through it in every direction. The soil, largely imbued with the products of putrefaction, is also extremely moist; many of the tomb-stones have sunk deeply in the earth. Here the peculiar putrefactive odour may be frequently distinguished,—as indeed it may in many of the burial places I have described.

The church is a very ancient one, of the gothic structure; in the centre, below the east window, is placed a marble tablet, which is known in the neighbourhood as the Fish and Ring (a fish and ring are cut on the top of the tablet.)

The following is a copy of the inscription engraved upon the tablet :—

" Here lieth interred the Body of Dame Rebecca Berry, the Wife of Thomas Elton, of Stratford Bow, who departed this life April 26th, 1696, aged 52.

" Come, ladies, you that would appear
  Like angels fair, come, dress you here ;
Come, dress you at this marble stone,
  And make that humble grace your own,
Which once adorn'd as fair a mind
  As e'er yet lodg'd in womankind.
So she was dress'd whose humble life
  Was free from pride, was free from strife ;
Free from all envious brawls and jars,
  Of human life the civil wars ;
These ne'er disturb'd her peaceful mind,
  Which still was gentle, still was kind ;
Her very looks, her garb, her mien,
  Disclos'd the humble soul within !
Trace her through every scene of life,
  View her as widow, virgin, wife ;
Still the same humble she appears,
  The same in youth, the same in years ;
The same in low and high estate,
  Ne'er vex'd with this, near mov'd with that.
Go, ladies now, and if you'd be
As fair, as great, as good as she,
Go learn of her humility."

MULBERRY CHAPEL, *Well Street, St. George's in the East.*—There are three vaults belonging to this chapel, one underneath the *chapel,* one underneath the *school* connected with it, and one underneath the *alms-houses.* They are all very full of bodies, particularly the two latter ; a great many of the coffins are in a very decayed state ; the smell from them is very offensive ; the neighbourhood is densely inhabited.

ELENORA, SWEDISH PROTESTANT CHURCH, in Princess Square.—The ground was given to Charles the XIIth of Sweden, and the church was built by his sister, Elenora, after whom it is named. The burial ground is full ; interment in it is discontinued. The grave digger, an old Swede, narrowly escaped with his life, on two occasions, from the falling in of the ground. There is a vault underneath the church, which is never opened, unless for burial ; the entrance is secured by a very heavy stone slab, which, after every funeral, is securely cemented down.

ST. GEORGE'S CHURCH, *Cannon Street, East.* —This is the parish church. The burial ground, which adjoins the church, is excessively crowded ; many of the tomb-stones have sunk into the ground. There are public and private vaults ; the former underneath the steps and entrance, the latter under the body of the church. The public vaults are greatly crowded, and in a loathsome state.

EBENEZER CHAPEL, *Ratcliff Highway.*—The burying ground is very small, but overcharged with dead; it is considered dangerous to open a grave; the neighbourhood is very populous. This is a *private ground.*

SHEEN'S BURIAL GROUND, *Commercial Road.* —This also is a *private* burying place. The proprietor of this ground is an undertaker. He has planted it with trees and shrubs, which are sufficiently attractive, but the ground is saturated with human putrescence.

SHADWELL CHURCH.—The ground adjoining the church is very full, and so also are the vaults underneath it.

TRINITY EPISCOPAL CHAPEL, *Cannon Street Road.*—The burying ground at the back of this chapel is large, and very much crowded. The fees are low; many of the Irish are buried here, and bodies are brought from very distant parishes; many of the grave stones have given way.

There is a *school room for children* at one end of the ground, built over a shed, in which are deposited pieces of broken-up coffin wood, tools, &c.

MARINER'S CHURCH, *Well Close Square.*—This was formerly used as a Danish place of worship, but has since been purchased by the Rev. — Smith, of Penzance. There is a burial ground adjoining the church, and a vault underneath it ; but this is now never used. The ground is very full ; many foreigners have been inhumed here.

BUNHILL FIELDS, *City Road.*—This old established Dissenting burial ground contains about seven acres. It was originally let on lease to a Mr. Tickell ; it was first opened in 1665. More than one hundred thousand interments are supposed to have taken place in it. The monument to the Rev. John Bunyan contains the following inscription :—

JOHN BUNYAN,
AUTHOR OF THE PILGRIM'S PROGRESS.
OBT. 31 AUG. 1688.
ÆT. 60.

Until a few years ago, the average annual number buried in this ground was about a thousand ; the fees were increased, and the number now averages about seven hundred.

ST. LUKE'S, *Old Street.*—There are three burying grounds belonging to this parish ; two adjoining the church, and the poor ground, in Bath Street. Those near the church are spacious ; some of the graves are very deep. The grave digger assured me, that he had often experienced the effects of the effluvia arising from the coffins, to an alarming extent, a frequent occurrence when coming suddenly upon a fresh grave, where the body had been kept too long before interment ; then the effluvium would penetrate through a foot and a half or two feet of earth, and frequently produced nausea and loathing of food. He stated that many accidents arose from neglect or carelessness; a grave partly dug and left exposed for a night would, for instance, become dangerous from the collection of " foul air."

The poor ground is at the back of the alms-houses, in Bath Street; an improved system of interment is adopted in this ground. The vaults underneath the church are less used than formerly, on account of the cemeteries round the metropolis, but the smell from these vaults is particularly offensive,—so much so, that I was informed by the Rev. Dr. Rice, the present Curate, that he never ventured to descend, but invariably performed the funeral rites whilst standing in the passage, at the top of the entrance to the vaults.

CLERKENWELL CHURCH.—There are four burying grounds belonging to this parish, besides a vault underneath the church; two of the grounds adjoin the church, a third is behind the prison, and the fourth, or poor ground, is in Ray Street, the entrance to which is through a private dwelling house, occupied by a broker.([1]) All these grounds are crowded, and in disorder; in the poor ground

([1]) It formerly was occupied by a butcher, named *Rope*, who had his slaughter-house and stable at the back, and immediately adjoining the burial ground. About fifteen years ago, during the residence of this man, it was discovered that several bodies had been exhumed and placed in the stable, close to the slaughter-house; the inhabitants of the vicinity were powerfully excited, and

little regard is paid to the depth of the graves, or the removal of the dead. In this filthy neighbourhood fever prevails, and poverty and wretchedness go hand-in-hand.

SPA FIELDS.—This ground was originally taken for a tea garden; the speculation failed, and a chapel was built upon it, in which some ministers of the Church of England preached. The Bishop refused to consecrate it, and it was ultimately bought by Lady Huntingdon; she inducted one of her Chaplains, and it is now much frequented. The burying ground is very large, but absolutely saturated with dead. ([1])

ST. JAMES'S BURYING GROUND, *Clerkenwell.*—This is a very extensive ground, and many of the lower Irish are buried here; the place appears excessively crowded. The mortality among children in this neighbourhood, within the last two months, has been very great. This will not occasion surprise when the locality of the burying ground, and the filth and wretchedness of the major part of the inhabitants are duly considered.

the man, who had for many years carried on an extensive business, was deservedly ruined, and driven in disgrace from the neighbourhood.

([1]) This place offers a difficult problem for solution;—no undertaker can explain it, excepting by a shrug of the shoulders. I can affirm, from frequent personal observation, that enormous numbers of dead have been deposited here.

St. Ann's, *Soho.*—There is only one burying ground belonging to this parish; it is walled in on the side next to Princes Street; close to this wall is the bone house; rotten coffin wood and fragments of bones are scattered about. Some graves are only partly filled up, and left in that state, intended, probably, for paupers. The ground is very full, and is considerably raised above its original level; it is overlooked by houses thickly inhabited. The inhabitants of the neighbourhood have frequently complained of the past and present condition of this place. The numbers of dead here are immense.

Elim Chapel, *Fetter Lane.*—This chapel has a vault underneath it, crowded with dead; it much resembles the state of Enon chapel. A report is currently circulated, that some time ago, water had forced a passage into this vault, and that the stench proceeding from it had produced injurious effects upon the health of the inhabitants in the immediate neighbourhood.

St. Saviour's Church, *Southwark.*—The burial ground adjoining the church is very full. The *poor ground,* called " *Cross Bones,*" in Red Cross Street, Union Street, Borough, also belongs to this parish. The greater portion of this ground has not been opened for some time past, in consequence of its very crowded state; ([1]) the remaining part, how-

([1]) On the 20th February last, a vestry meeting was holden " for the purpose of considering the propriety of re-opening the Cross Bones burying ground." The ground had been closed about

N

ever, is still used for interments, many of the poor Irish are buried in it. Two charity schools, one for boys and the other for girls, are built at the west end, in Union Street, the back parts of which run into this ground.

There are two vaults belonging to this church, one called the Great Vault, underneath the body of the church. The coffins are piled one upon another; some, which contain branches of the same family, are chained together. All the bodies placed in this vault are buried in lead,—a condition never deviated from. When this vault is opened a fire is always kept burning. On one occasion I accompanied the grave digger to this vault; he received a caution from the sextoness, and hesitated for some time before opening the door; he observed that " he should know, directly he opened the place,

two years *(the time generally allowed for the destruction of the bodies !)* and it was moved that it be re-opened; the mover of the resolution stating, that in consequence of the aversion generally manifested to bury in what is named the " Irish corner," many bodies were taken out of the parish to be buried. *This corner, however, had been cleared, and room made for about a thousand bodies.* One gentleman argued that " if the graves had been made deeper, hundreds more corpses might have been buried there." Another admitted that it really was too bad to bury within eighteen inches of the surface, in such a crowded neighbourhood; and it was even hinted that " *the clearing*," viz. the digging up and the removal *of the decayed fragments of flesh and bones, with the pieces of coffin, &c. would be the best course, were it not for the additional expense.*"

The *funds* of the vestry and the *health* of the living were here placed in opposite scales,—the former had its preponderance.

whether there was danger." In descending, he carried a lighted candle at arm's-length; he then called out, "there is no danger." The place is extremely damp, and gives out a most offensive smell.

Another vault, called the Bishop's vault, runs underneath the church yard. Light and air are admitted from the burial ground, through an iron grating. The entrance to this vault is through the "Ladye Chapel;" the roof is arched over with brick-work. The coffins are piled upon one another, but the burying in lead is left to the option of the party concerned in the funeral; the smell here is more offensive than in the larger vault.

EWER STREET CHAPEL AND BURYING GROUND, at the bottom of Union Street, Borough.—The burying ground appears to have been raised nearly six feet from the original surface, and is literally surcharged with dead; it is now closed, and presents a very repulsive aspect. It might be instructive to know the number of bodies here inhumed; perhaps,—but dead men tell no tales,—the exhumed might present a formidable array. The vicinity is disgustingly dirty.

DEADMAN'S PLACE.—This burying ground is near to Ewer Street, and is equally surcharged with dead,—the name befits the appearance.(¹)

(¹) Tradition says it took its name from the number of the dead interred there in the great plague, soon after the Restoration.— (*Pennant.*)

ST. OLAVE'S BURYING GROUND, bottom of Tooley Street, consecrated in 1583.—A grave digger, named Stewart, died of typhus, in May last. His wife was buried with him, who also died of typhus.

ST. JOHN'S BURYING GROUND.—This ground is much crowded. The grave digger appeared fully sensible of the dangers to be apprehended in the practice of his avocation.

CATHOLIC CHAPEL, *Dock Head.*—Underneath is a vault open to the air by iron gratings; the grave digger had experienced very annoying effects, from striking upon a coffin buried a short time previous.

BERMONDSEY CHURCH YARD is very much crowded; many of the tomb stones are sunk into the ground, and the whole site may be said to be covered with monuments. The two following are singular :—

" In memory of Mary, first wife of William Collier, who died 3d of August, 1815, aged 60 years, after having been afflicted 19 years and 7 months, with the rheumatism, and was under 19 Doctors, &c. without any good effect. She was buried in Bunhill Fields."

" Here lie the remains of Susannah Wood, wife of Mr. James Wood, of the Kent Road, Mathematical Instrument Maker, who, after a long and painful illness, which she bore with the greatest fortitude, departed this life the 16th June, 1810, in the 58th year of her age. She was tapped 97 times, and had 461 gallons of water taken from her, without ever lamenting her case, or fearing the operation."

Ground in immediate proximity to this place

is advertised to be "let on lease" for building purposes.

New Bunhill Fields.—This burying ground is situate in the New Kent Road; it is a private speculation, and belongs to Mr. Martin, an undertaker.

It has many attractions for survivors ; the fees are low, the grounds are walled round and well watched, and the superintendent of the place resides upon the spot. At the entrance of the ground a chapel has been erected; it belongs to the Wesleyan connexion; under this chapel, arched with strong brick-work, is a spacious vault, containing about eighteen hundred coffins.([1]) Iron gratings are placed on each side of the vault, and its entrance is by steps, through rather an extensive door-way. It appears that the original proprietor of the place was named Hoole. Two coffins, one containing his remains, and the other, stated to contain the remains of his daughter, are placed in the bottom of the vault, at the upper end, on the left hand side of it, enclosed with iron railings. The other coffins are placed in rows, one above the other ; some of them distinguished by small plates, placed upon the end or sides of the coffins, having particular inscriptions. The following struck me as deserving notice :—

MRS. MARY JANE MURRAY,

OBIIT JULY 3, 1838,

AGED 36 YEARS.

" I have given the lovely to earth's embrace,
She has taken the fairest of Beauty's race."

([1]) There are not more, I believe, than twelve bodies placed in lead out of the entire number.

A strong ammoniacal odour pervades this vault; it is not so offensive as that which I have experienced in most other depositories of this description; this I attribute, to the constant transmission of the noxious vapours, (through open iron gratings) to the circumambient atmosphere.

The burial ground and vault, it appears, have been employed, for the purposes of interment, about eighteen years, during which, not less than ten thousand bodies have been inhumed and deposited, within this " narrow spot of earth," and the vault connected with it. Yet, around this tainted atmosphere, many houses are erected and boards are placed offering ground to be let upon building leases!

LAMBETH CHURCH.—This is close to the Bishop's Palace. There is a vault under the church, and a burying ground adjoining to it, both of which are for private or family graves. The ground is very full; it is contiguous to the river, and the soil is very damp; many of the tomb-stones have sunk into the earth.

At a short distance from the church is another burying ground, belonging to the parish; it is divided into the upper, middle, and lower grounds. It is very much crowded, and the tomb-stones are deeply sunk in the earth; the state of the ground has rendered it necessary to discontinue the practice of interment,—bones are scattered about, and a part of the ground has been raised. The neighbourhood is thickly populated ; the soil is very moist, and water flows in at the depth of four feet.

St. Margaret's, *Westminster*. (¹)—There are two burying grounds belonging to this parish, one near the Abbey, adjoining the church, and the other in the Broadway, Westminster. The latter was formerly used as a burying place for soldiers ; that practice has, however, been discontinued,—the ground is excessively crowded ; *funerals are very frequent.* The ground behind the church, is too full to admit of increase, with propriety or safety.

There are *two other burying grounds* near to this spot, belonging to St. John's, *Westminster*, the *old* and the *new ground;* the latter filled so fast, that the parish authorities were obliged to employ the old ground again. Soldiers are now buried here.

St. John's Burying Ground, *Westminster*, is very spacious and over-crowded; the churchwardens have been obliged to give up a part of the ground, for the interment of the poor, which had formerly been set apart, for the more fortunate. The soil here is very damp, and, at a shallow depth, the water flows in abundantly ; the depth of the graves varies from four to eight feet.

Romney Street Chapel, close to St. John's burial ground.—This is a Baptist place of worship, with vaults underneath, not unlike those under Buckingham chapel, but not so large. The smell

(¹) See the remarks from the *Quarterly Review,* on the condition of this ground, in the year 1814.

from the vaults is exceedingly offensive, and produces a feeling of nausea.

BUCKINGHAM CHAPEL, situated in Palace Street, about three minutes' walk from Buckingham Palace. There are two vaults and a burying ground belonging to this chapel; one of the vaults is *underneath very large school rooms for boys and girls,* (¹) and the other is *underneath the chapel;* the entrance to these vaults, is through a trap-door, in the passage, dividing the school rooms from the chapel; steps lead to the bottom of the building; on the right, is the vault underneath the schools. When I visited this place a body had recently been interred, and the effluvium from it was particularly annoying. The vault is supported on wooden pillars, and there is only one grating, which fronts the street, to admit light and air; the floors of the school rooms, white-washed on the under surface, form the roof or ceiling of the vault—it is no difficult matter to see the children in the lower school room from this vault, *as there are apertures in the boards sufficiently large to admit the light from above.* This place is spacious, but very low;—the vault on the left, under the chapel, is about the same size as that under the schools, though much lower. I was assured that the ground was so full of bodies, that there was difficulty in allotting a grave; the roof of this vault, is formed by the under surface of the floor of the chapel; it is white-washed, the light

(¹) Some hundreds of children here receive their daily education.

passes through it; the smell emitted from this place is very offensive. In the vault underneath the chapel there are piles of bodies placed in lead; the upper ones are within a few inches of the wooden floor.

On a level with the chapel, and behind it and the school rooms, is the burial ground, which is much crowded,—most of the graves being full 7 feet deep, and nearly filled to the surface, with the dead; the ground is raised, more than six feet from the original level,—formed only by the debris of mortality. No funerals are permitted on a Sunday.

Interments are allowed, in either vault, *in lead or not,—if not in lead, two wooden cases are required, a shell, and an outer coffin.*

I could not but feel surprised that in the very atmosphere of the Palace, such a nuisance as I have just described—a nuisance, pouring out the deadly emanations of human putrescence, should be allowed to exist—still more so, that it should be permitted daily to increase; *it is now exposed*, when will it be *denounced?*—surely the guardians of Her Majesty's health, will not risk the consequences of neglect. *Precedent* would justify even a *summary* interference,—so thought, and so acted, the heads of Royalty in former times. The letter from Henry the Eighth, to the " Abot of Westmynster," dated the 12th November, 1535, speaks home truths in quaint language. The following extract, while it amuses the antiquarian, will prove, how jealously, even the transmission of the dead, through the precincts of the Court was accustomed to be regarded :—

Thys is the trewe Coppie of the Kyng's Grace most gracious Letters delivered unto the Abot of Westmynster.

REVEREND Father in God, Ryght Trustie, and welbeloved, We gret you well. Forasmuch as by natural inclynacion we be bounden to provide for the salve garde of our p'sonage and Majestie, and for the p'sonage of our most excllente and most intierly beloved Lady ou^r Queene, as of ou^r most derre daughter or prynces, and of all other nobill subjects, famylie, and trayne, and that pte ys so that ou^r Mano^r of Westmynster ys nowe site and situat as in the myddes of tew parishes, that is to say, of Saynte Margarett, where ye have jurydyxon ordynary, and of Saynte Martyn in the Felds, where y^e be psons and prepetaries; and that sondrye and often tymes, by recorse of much people resortynge from sondry parties of the world, unto us often tymes great sykness dothe raigne in both those pishes, by reason whereof the corpses of such inhabytances and dwellers wythin the bounds, lymets, and psynk of the pishes of St Martyn and that be of the pishe of Saynt Margarett, when they do dye of any dysease, as pestelence, agew, or any other contagiose syknes, the same corpses of the dede parsons be brought and borne yerly and lat, nyghtly and daylye, throught oure said Mano^r, to there bery all and p'ishe churche to be beryed, to no lyttel jeperdy of us and of all other ou^r subjects and trayne, as well as their goinge and comyng, by the infecte parsons (') accompanying the dede p'rsons and bodyes as by the infeccion of their clothes and otherwysse, in tyme of visitacion of such as chuse to fall syke: We, in consideracion thereof, & ffor lawful remedye in this behalfe to be had, weell and praye you, and also commande you havynge ordynary power, & being as before ys said psons & p'petareys of bothe those churches and to whom, and our Monas-

(¹) More than three hundred years have elapsed since the above opinions were recorded. What progress has science made on this particular subject since that period? Has it, in this country at least, determined whether " dede bodyes," left to the uncontrolled keeping of the survivors,—" waked" by the Irish, or allowed " to sleep" many days above the surface by the English,—do or do not exert injurious action upon the living? Are there not in low crowded neighbourhoods enough of terrestrial and corporeal exhalations? There are, indeed, sufficient sources of disease without the addition of others that might be avoided.

terye of Westmynster, bothe those churches be appat and incorporat', and callying also unto you in our name the Vicar of Saynt Martyn's, that yᵉ together sall and go to such cocitation, composicion, and devise betwyxt you, by the advice, decre, sentens, and confymacion ordenaire, of those that have enterst in this behalfe, as shall stand wᵗ right and equitie, so that all and the hole inhabytants, now p'rshioners, of your pishe of Saynt Margarett, dwelling wᵗin the saide lymytts, bondes & pcynts of Saynt Martyns aforesaid, and by northe and est our saide Manoʳ be separat, dyvided, and dymembered from the pishe and pyssheoners of Saynt Margaretts; & that they and every one of them so dwelling from henceforthe be ordered, deputed, decreed, lymyted, and taken ffor p'issheners of Saynt Martyns, and ther to here all other devyne s'rvice, & to receive all there sacraments & sacramentals, as well beryall as other, and that at Saynt Martyns they do paye all ther tythes, rights, and oblations wᵗ offryng, as oder the p'rshoners of Saynt Martyns now there doth p'petually, demandyng, also, all such youʳ composicion, decre, and sentens in this behalfe, to be made to be put in execusion, and commandying the same in our name to be published in both those churches, and inviolatˡʸ to be observed by the inhabytants aforesaid, wytheout any contradiction from henceforth, not faylynge hereof, wythe dylygent expedicion, as yᵉ entend our hyght, pleasure, and beare good zeale towards us and others in these permysses. Geven at ouʳ Manoʳ of Westmynster, the xij of November, in the xxvj yere of ouʳ raigne.

Enough, nay, more than enough, has now been stated, to show the dangerous state, and deleterious influence, of the " grave yard;" the exposition I have given, will, it is presumed, awaken even the inert, from their dreams of security, and stimulate the active and benevolent, to assiduous and persevering efforts, to eradicate, from the proximity of their dwellings, one of the many, perhaps the most, fruitful causes of disease, impairing or destroying the health, and, consequently, the happiness of their fellow men.

ON THE GROSS ABUSES—THE DANGEROUS, OF-
FENSIVE, AND DEMORALISING CONSEQUENCES
OF THE PRESENT MODES OF INTERMENT.

In the preceding pages, I have, necessarily, touched upon some of the more prominent abuses, of the
" grave yard;" and my readers are already prepared, to anticipate much that may be now advanced.
Were I to indulge in the expression of feelings,
which the consideration of this part of my subject,
has, from time to time, excited, I might subject myself to the imputation of attempting to influence the
passions, rather than of endeavouring to convey important and useful information.

Decently to dispose of the dead, and vigilantly
to secure their remains from violation, are among
the first duties of society; our domestic endear-
ments—our social attachments—our national prepossessions, respect and sanctify the resting places
of our forefathers; the most barbarous of mankind,
would burn with indignation, at beholding the last
remains of a beloved relative exposed, mangled, or
mutilated :(¹) and yet, among us, in a moral and

(¹) At present thousands do not "die like men,"—there is too
much reason to add—that they " sink below, like brutes ;" and the
noblest animal is treated, by his fellows infinitely worse, in his state
of non-resistance, than the commonwealth of animals, termed by
man instinctive, treat their dead.

My friend, Mr. O. Smith has furnished me with an instance in
illustration of this remark :—

" Walking on Coombe Down, near Bath, some years since, he
observed a sheep busily employed in arranging a piece of old canvas ; his curiosity was excited by the apparent anxiety of the crea-
ture ; he stepped up, threw the canvas some distance, and found

Christian country, the abode of the dead is openly violated—its deposits are sacrilegiously disturbed, and ejected—the tender solicitudes of survivors, are cruelly sported with, and the identity of relationship is destroyed,—so eager, indeed, is the haste, to dispossess previous occupants, that time is not even allowed, for the *gradual* dissipation of decaying human putrescence; this is eliminated in gaseous profusion, contaminating, as it circulates, the habitations of the living.

Whence this rude invasion of the tomb? How can we reconcile, the previous anxieties of survivors,

he had uncovered a dead lamb; he retired some paces, the sheep brought back the canvas in her mouth, and, very carefully, again covered over the object of its solicitude and affection."

" To Dr. Williams, who did carry me into his garden, where he hath abundance of grapes : and he did show me how a dog that he hath do kill all the cats that come thither to kill his pigeons, and do afterwards bury them ; and do it with so much care, that they shall be quite covered ; that if the tip of the tail hangs out he will take up the cat again, and dig the hole deeper ; which is very strange ; and he tells me, that he do believe that he hath killed above one hundred cats."—(Pepy's Diary, Sept. 11, 1661.)

Every school boy will remember with what diligence birds exert themselves to eject the dead from their nests. I have seen rooks and starlings labouring, apparently with the greatest anxiety, to get rid of a dead offspring; and in some instances, where they could not effect their object, they have left the remaining young ones to their fate.

I have often noticed a couple of sturdy bees, bring out a dead one from the hive, and support it for some distance, before allowing it to fall to the earth. These little creatures, thus anxious to remove their dead, from the neighbourhood of their dwellings, offer, in their instinctive efforts, a severe commentary on the conduct of, and a lesson to, the " proud reasoner, man."

to secure a respectable interment, with the subsequent unconcern, neglect, or abandonment of the localities of the dead? I shall not presume to solve these questions; however, I cannot help thinking, that the depredations of the " grave yard" are comparatively disregarded, from a feeling and a desire common to every man,—a feeling of unwillingness to believe, that his own friends have been disturbed, and, a natural desire to avoid the renewal of melancholy reminiscences. " All men think all men mortal but themselves." This self delusion, is carried yet further; for, while every man readily sympathizes with others, at the disturbance of their dead; he believes his own depository secure, and his future repose inviolable.

But who are most deeply interested in the sanctity of the sepulchre, viewing it as a mere resting place? Not the *noble*, not the *wealthy* (the former will rest with his fathers, the latter *may* purchase his exemption from disturbance), but, the *middle man*, the tradesman, the artisan, and the mechanic, the man who labours from the rising to the setting sun, to provide for the wants and the comforts of existence, and to lay by the means of decently interring his remains;—and *the very poor*; in the one case, the watchfulness of survivors presents some, although a merely temporary check, to the disturbance of the grave; in the other, the caprice of office determines the duration.

In this country we have very seldom to complain of extreme haste, in survivors, to perform the funeral rites. Custom is in favour of delay sufficiently great, to preclude all apprehensions of premature interment; but periods have happened, and in times too not far distant, in which persons, supposed to be dead, have been hurriedly conveyed to their long home, when, possibly, life was not extinct, and when recovery might have been effected, by the employment of judicious and persevering efforts.

The following observations upon the subject of "premature interment," are deserving consideration:—

" On many occasions, in all places, too much precipitation attends this last office; or if not precipitation, a neglect of due precautions, in regard to the body in general; indeed, the most improper treatment that can be imagined, is adopted, and many a person made to descend into the grave, before he has sighed his last breath: ancient and modern authors, leave us no doubt, respecting the dangers, or misconduct of such precipitation. It must appear astonishing, that the attention of mankind has been, after all, so little roused, by an idea, the most terrible that can be conceived, on this side of eternity. According to present usage, as soon as the semblance of death appears, the chamber of the sick is deserted by friends, relatives, and physicians; and the apparently dead, though frequently living body, is committed to the management of an ignorant and unfeeling nurse, whose care extends no further than laying the limbs straight, and securing her accustomed perquisites. The bed clothes are immediately removed, and the body is exposed to the air. This, when cold, must extinguish any spark of life that may remain, and which, by a different treatment, might have been kindled into flame; or it may only continue to repress it, and the unhappy person afterwards revive, amidst the horrors of the tomb.

" The difference between the end of a weak life, and the commencement of death, is so small, and the uncertainty of the signs of the latter is so well established, that we can scarcely suppose undertakers capable of distinguishing an apparent from a real death. Animals which sleep during winter, show no signs of life; in this case circulation is only suspended; but were it annihilated, the vital spark does not so easily lose its action as the fluids of the body, and the principle of life, which long survives the appearance of death, may re-animate a body, in which the action of all the organs, seems to be at an end. But how difficult is it to determine, whether this principle may not be revived? It has been found impossible to recal to life some animals, suffocated by mephitic vapours, though they appeared less affected than others, which have revived. Coldness, heaviness of the body, a leaden livid colour, with a yellowness in the visage, are all very uncertain signs. M. Zimmerman observed them all, upon the body of a criminal, who fainted through the dread of that punishment, which he had merited. He was shaken, dragged about, and turned in the same manner as dead bodies are, without the least signs of resistance, and yet, at the end of twenty-four hours, he was recalled to life, by means of the volatile alkali."

The following cases bear directly upon this subject, and are well worth perusal:—

" Cardinal Somaglia was seized with a severe illness, from extreme grief; he fell into a state of syncope, which lasted so long, that the persons around him thought him dead. Preparations were instantly made to embalm his body, before the putrefactive process should commence, in order that he might be placed in a leaden coffin, in the family vault. The operator had scarcely penetrated into his chest, when the heart was seen to beat. The unfortunate patient, who was returning to his senses at that moment, had still sufficient strength to push away the knife of the surgeon, but too late, for the lung had been mortally wounded, and the patient died in a most lamentable manner."—*Journal de Rouen*, Aug. 5, 1837.

" Mr. B. inhabitant of Poitiers, fell suddenly into a state resembling death; every means for bringing him back to life were used without interruption; from continued dragging, his two little fingers were dislocated, and the soles of his feet were burnt, but all these having produced no sensation in him, he was thought decidedly dead. As they were on the point of placing him in his coffin, some one recommended that he should be bled in both arms and feet, at the same time, which was immediately done, and with such success, that, to the astonishment of all, he recovered from his apparent state of death. When he had entirely recovered his senses, he declared that he had heard every word that had been said, and that his only fear was, that he would be buried alive."— (Memoire sur les inhumations précipitées, par J. B. Vigné, Paris, 1839.)

" A lady was attacked with the plague; she was considered dead, and buried in a large pit. When the persons returned to bury some other bodies, they found her living; she was taken home, and afterwards recovered."

" A frightful case of premature interment occurred not long since, at Tonneins, in the Lower Garonne. The victim, a man in the prime of life, had only a few shovelfuls of earth thrown into his grave, when an indistinct noise was heard to proceed from his coffin. The grave digger, terrified beyond description, instantly fled to seek assistance, and some time elapsed before his return ; when the crowd, which had by this time collected in considerable numbers round the grave, insisted on the coffin being opened. As soon as the first boards had been removed, it was ascertained, beyond a doubt, that the occupant had been interred alive. His countenance was frightfully contracted with the agony he had undergone; and in his struggles, the unhappy man had forced his arms completely out of the winding sheet, in which they had been securely enveloped. A physician, who was on the spot, opened a vein, but no blood followed. The sufferer was beyond the reach of art.—(*Sunday Times*, Dec. 30, 1838.)

During the awful visitation of the spasmodic cholera, in 1831-32, the alarm of the inhabitants, in crowded neighbourhoods, more particularly—was naturally very great; and in some instances, we may reasonably fear, interments were prematurely made.

A very shallow grave was excavated in a burying ground, which had long been filled with dead, in the centre of an extremely populous neighbourhood; remonstrance was made, by persons dwelling in the houses, surrounding this ground, many of whom had witnessed the perpetration of some of the most disgusting scenes. The Magistrates of the district were applied to, but with very little success. One of the functionaries of the parish threatened " to bury the next cholera patient under the windows of the principal remonstrant."

I was informed, by a very respectable undertaker,

that in many instances, " as soon as life had departed," even in ten minutes afterwards, many bodies were covered with lime, screwed down, and thrown into trenches, each containing from thirty to fifty bodies, and sometimes even more.

It appears from an official return, made to the House of Commons, in the year 1833, that " in the parishes and places within the London bills of mortality, and of Chelsea, Kensington, Saint Mary-le-Bone, Paddington, and St. Pancras, in the county of Middlesex," 32,412 interments took place in the burying places of the Establishment, exclusive of those belonging to the Dissenters, Jews, and Catholics.(¹) From this return the following numbers are taken, viz:—

All Saints, Poplar, 456; St. Andrews, Holborn, 820,; St. Anne, Limehouse, 396; St. Anne, Westminster, 494; Christ Church, Spital Fields, 564;

(¹) I have not been able to procure any satisfactory accounts of the numbers interred in burying grounds unconnected with the Established Church. By some parties *information was refused*, by others the records of the place were stated to have been *lost or neglected*, and in some cases the *parties most interested in* SUPPRESSING, *had alone the power to communicate.*

There are, in various parts of the metropolis, about 450 places of worship, of which nearly 200 belong to the Establishment; there are 47 for Baptists, 6 for the Society of Friends, upwards of 100 for Independents, 32 for Wesleyan Methodists, 4 for Swedenborgians, 6 for Unitarians, 4 for Welsh Calvinists, and numerous others for different classes of Protestant Dissenters. There are, also, 9 chapels in connection with the Church of Scotland, 14 Roman Catholic chapels, 7 synagogues, and 18 foreign Protestant churches and chapels.—(Lewis' Topographical Dictionary, p. 154.)

Christ Church, Surrey, 540; St. Clement Danes, 516; St. Dunstan, Stepney, 703; St. George, Hanover Square, 1510; Saint George, Middlesex, 708; St. George, Southwark, 943; St. Giles in the Fields, 1642; St. James, Clerkenwell, 842; St. James, Westminster, 803; St. Leonard, Shoreditch, 963; Saint Luke, Chelsea, 1033; St. Luke, Old Street, 593; St. Margaret, Westminster, 930; St. Martin in the Fields, 565; St. Mary, Islington, 796; St. Mary, Lambeth, 1427; St. Mary, Newington, 547; St. Mary, Rotherhithe, 454; St. Mary, Whitechapel, 557; St. Mary-le-Bone, 3040; St. Matthew, Bethnal Green, 1054; St. Pancras, 1769; St. Paul, Covent Garden, 106; St. Saviour, Southwark, 590.

From *official* documents ([1]) it also appears that the number of bodies buried in the metropolis

From 1741 to 1765, inclusive, were 588,523

1766 ... 1792..................... 605,832

1793 ... 1813..................... 402,595

1814 ... 1837..................... 508,162

_____

2,105,112

_____

In a communication from J. Finlaison, Esq. Actuary of the National Debt Office, to T. H. Lister, Esq. Registrar General, dated February 2, 1839,

([1]) I am perfectly convinced that from many private burial grounds, in low and crowded neighbourhoods, where the lowness of the fees has occasioned an immense influx of funerals, *no returns whatever have been made,* or returns purposely inaccurate, have been furnished. The returns from some places I could name would be instructive.

it is stated, that the *annual number* of burials in England and Wales, upon an average of five years, is 335,968.

Can we then wonder that disease and death are making frightful ravages, when millions of human bodies are putrefying in the very midst of us?

In the description of many of the metropolitan burying grounds, it will be seen that by far the greater number are crowded even to excess; (¹) this certainly ought not to have been permitted,— the moment it appeared that the space allotted for interment, was occupied—*that* moment the ground should have been closed, and other asylums set apart for the interment of the dead : an infringement upon the occupancy of the unresisting tenant violates the property of survivors, and desecrates the sanctity of the sepulchre. Men pay *funeral*

(¹) " In large towns in England, and more especially in the metropolis, it has become more difficult to find room for the dead than for the living. The Commissioners for the Improvements in Westminster, reported to Parliament, in 1814, that St. Margaret's church yard could not, consistently with the health of the neighbourhood, be used much longer as a burying ground, ' for that it was with the greatest difficulty a vacant place could, at any time, be found for strangers; the family graves, generally, would not admit of more than one interment, and many of them were then too full for the reception of any member of the family to which they belonged.' There are many church yards in which the soil has been raised several feet above the level of the adjoining street, by the constant accumulation of mortal matter; and there are others in which the ground is actually probed with a borer before a grave is opened ! In these things the most barbarous savages might reasonably be shocked at our barbarity.—(Quarterly Review, Sept. 1819, p. 380.)

dues under an implied assurance that the " dead" shall be " respected."

It is well known, that formerly, considerable alarm was manifested that the grave would be robbed of its deposits by the intrusion of the " resurrectionist." An Act of the Legislature had the effect of destroying the temptation to purloin the dead, but the grave is still insecure. Grounds, accustomed to be held sacred, are unceremoniously cleared under *official* superintendence; and that too with such ruthless indifference and wanton publicity, that even passers-by complain of the indecent profanation.

———

Having explained the nature, and pointed out the dangers of grave-yard emanations,—having stated, also, that the burying grounds of the metropolis are literally saturated with the dead, I shall now show by what arrangements the superfluity is reduced, and room made for subsequent interments; and in doing this, I shall restrict myself to a brief enumeration of some of the particulars.

The means employed to effect the purposes contemplated, consist in what, by the grave diggers, is called "management."

In this " management" of the ground, former occupancy is disregarded; coffins are remorselessly broken through, and their contents heaped together, in wild confusion, or scattered carelessly over the surface, exposed to " insult lewd and wantonness."

Great expense is frequently incurred in funerals; the encasement is often strongly made, and highly ornamented; it is not difficult to account for the fact that second-hand " coffin furniture," nails, more especially, (¹) may be found by the hundred weight, at many of the " dealers in marine stores," nor can we wonder that *coffin wood has*

(¹) This point is established by the following extract from the *Morning Post*, Monday, Oct. 14, 1839 :—

INDECENT DISINTERMENT OF DEAD BODIES.—Since Friday, a good deal of excitement has prevailed in the neighbourhood of Globe Lane, Mile-end, in consequence of the interference of the police to prevent the indecent disinterment of bodies in the burial ground behind Globe Fields Chapel. It appeared that Mr. Poole, a clerk in the service of the Eastern Counties Railway Company, being stationed on that part of the railroad which runs close to the burial ground in question, had observed two men and a boy exhuming the bodies buried in one part of the ground, and hurling them, in the most indecent manner, and indiscriminately, into a deep hole, which they had previously made at another part; and considering such a proceeding as somewhat extraordinary, as well as exceedingly indecent, he felt it to be his duty to call at the police station-house, in the Mile-end Road, and give information of what he had witnessed. Inspector M'Craw, accompanied by sergeants Parker and Shaw, K 10 and 3, in consequence proceeded to the burial ground in question, and as they were about to enter, they met a lad with a bag of bones and a quantity of nails, which he said he was going to sell. On examining them, the nails were evidently those which had been taken out of coffins, and the bones seemed to be those of human beings, but the lad denied that they were so, though he acknowledged the nails to have been taken from the coffins. The inspector and sergeants then proceeded to an obscure corner of the ground, and found there a great number of bodies, packed one upon another, in a very deep grave which had been dug to receive them, *and the uppermost coffin was not more than seven or eight inches, at the utmost, from the surface. The breast-plate and nails were removed from*

been extensively used as an ordinary fuel, in low neighbourhoods,—this fact I lately proved.—The products of *ordinary* combustion are sufficiently poisonous.([1]) The gases produced by the decomposition of the dead, are partially soluble in water; and a fatty pellicle is instantly formed in large quantity. The wood, saturated with these dissolved gases, and used as fuel, must diffuse, in addition to the exhalations constantly given off from bodies in vaults, and on the earth's surface, vast volumes of gaseous poison. What causes can have led to the employment of

the lid, so that they could at once remove the latter, and from the appearance of the body, as well as of the coffin, it appeared to be the remains of a person above the middle rank of life, and to have been interred about a month or six weeks. On making inquiries, it appeared that the ground was the property of an undertaker, residing in the neighbourhood of Bishopsgate Street; that owing to the low rate of fees, and affording a protection against resurrection men, by being surrounded by high walls, a great number of burials took place; *but as few would select the remote corner as a place of rest for their friends or relations, it was used for the purpose of removing the bodies of those buried in the better and more crowded part of the ground to make room for others.* The officers said that the dreadful stench emitted from the half-decomposed bodies, placed in the hole before mentioned, was sufficient to engender disease in the neighbourhood, upon which the men immediately set about covering them.

([1]) The importation of coals into the port of London was as follows:—

	SHIPS.	TONS.
In 1836	9,162	2,398,352
1837	8,720	2,626,997
1838	9,003	2,581,085

this dangerous—this disgusting fuel? what causes can have operated in compelling men, calling themselves Christians, to merge into a condition lower than that of brutes?   I will answer these questions, —warmth constitutes one of the most essential necessaries of life.   A kind Providence has given us inexhaustible stores of natural fuel; in many parts of the provinces excellent coal can be bought at eleven shillings per ton,—in London upwards of thirty shillings are demanded and paid.   It would be a libel on my countrymen were I to admit, that if this article was placed within their means of purchase, they would use, as a substitute, wood frequently saturated with human putrescence,—their "poverty, and not their will consents." The necessity for disposing of the coffin-wood (another result of the crowded state of the grounds), has led to its being given away, or sold in large quantities; the bodies, more easily destructible, are got rid of in various ways,—at some places lime is used.

The present Lord Mayor, the Rt. Hon. Sir S. Wilson, has fearlessly, and perseveringly, attacked the monopoly of this necessary of life; in his humane and patriotic efforts, he has the best wishes of every good and benevolent man, and the prayers of the poor for his success; a considerable reduction in the price of coal will destroy one of the temptations to violate the tomb,—a practice most shocking in itself, and highly injurious to all concerned.

In a burying ground, in Southwark, an application was made

for a grave; the grave digger said, " there was no room, except for a relative, and only through management could room be made!" He was interrogated concerning his " management."—He replied " he would be a fool to tell any one how he did it." It was observed to him, that the place appeared to be dreadfully crowded, and it was feared there was not sufficient depth. "Well," observed the man, " we can just give a covering to the body."

In making a grave, a body, partly decomposed, was dug up, and placed on the surface, at the side, slightly covered with earth; a mourner stepped upon it,—the loosened skin peeled off, he slipped forward, and had nearly fallen into the grave.

At another place, amongst a heap of rubbish, a young woman recognised the finger of her mother, who had been buried there a short time previous.

A poor widow, to evidence her affection for her departed husband, had seriously diminished her resources, to defray the funeral expenses; the coffin was covered with black cloth, and was some time after identified by the maker of it,—it was nearly covered with lime.

An undertaker, who had the charge of a funeral, went with a friend into the vault of a chapel; a coffin, recently deposited, was taken under his arm with the greatest ease; his friend, doubting, poised the coffin, and was affected to tears, from the conviction that the body had been removed. Several other coffins were in the same condition.

The workmen, in digging a grave in the burying ground of a chapel, much frequented, broke in upon a common sewer, and deposited the coffin there; the brother of the deceased insisted upon its removal; he compelled the workmen to place the body in the vault until another grave was dug; then dared them to remove it, and cautioned them not again to dig a grave for a human being, *entering the common sewer.*

The extract from an important examination before Sir C. Hunter, and the case immediately following it, mutually illustrate each other :—

" A man was charged before Sir Claudius Hunter (20th March, 1839), at Guildhall, with having in his possession some portions of leaden coffins, which had been stolen from the public vaults of Shoreditch Church.

" Sir C. Hunter asked if there was any additional evidence as to the coffin lead ?

" The vestry clerk said there was only one fact, that on one of the cases from which the lead coffin had been stolen, and which now contained the corpse, there was the name of the deceased, corresponding with one of the plates produced, as having been traced to Joseph's.

" Sir C. Hunter observed, that the sanctuary of the dead ought not to be invaded with impunity. The temptation to steal our bodies had been removed by the Legislature ; but now the love of gain *tempted persons to steal our coffins.*"

In the vaults of a church centrally situate, the burying ground of which is, on the surface, in a most disgusting condition, a nobleman, and several other persons of distinction, had found their last resting-place.

In the year —, a rumour arose in the parish, that the rights of sepulture had been grossly violated ; enquiries were instituted,— men were employed to replace the bodies in the shells that were left, and from which the lead had been stolen ; a hole was dug, into which the remainder of the bodies were thrown. The grave digger was privately examined before a magistrate ; it was found that any proceedings against him would implicate others. The affair was hushed up, and the vault, which had undergone a thorough clearance, was thus again made available for the purposes of interment, —again, perhaps, to be subjected to a similar purgation, when the cupidity of the grave digger may be in the ascendant, *or the want of room shall require it.*

One of these men told me, that " some of the bodies were comparatively fresh, and that the flesh of others was reduced to a brown and horribly fetid pulp, which left the bones on the slightest touch ;" but that no serious accident occurred, which can be accounted for by the fact—that the putrefactive process, attended by the evolution of gas, had gone by.

Four coffins, out of upwards of fifty, alone escaped these brutal depredators of the dead,—that which contained the remains of the nobleman, which it was expected would rest ultimately in ——, according to his last wish, and three others, secured by strong chains, passing through their handles at each end ; these were padlocked, and the keys were kept by the survivors.

It is well known to those engaged in burying the dead, that when leaden coffins are employed, the expansive force of the gas,(¹) and the consequent bulging out of the coffin, compels the workmen frequently to " tap" it,(²) that the gas may escape ;

(¹) The expansive force of the gas, formed during the process of decomposition, is illustrated in the following instance :—

The beloved daughter of a clergyman having died, he was anxious to preserve the body above ground, that he might have the melancholy satisfaction of viewing this " mouldering piece of clay." The body was first embalmed by a surgeon, one of my personal friends, and then put into a shell ; a leaden coffin received these, and a glass window was made in the top of the lead coffin. These were enclosed in a handsome mahogany coffin, " with a lid, that opened and shut." The day after the corpse was put in, the glass in the lead coffin broke ; it was replaced by another, which also broke ; and then a thick plate glass was put into an iron frame, soldered to the lead, which stood, and is now in the vestry of —— church !

(²) This is done by boring a hole with a gimlet ; a jet of gas instantly passes through the aperture, and this, when ignited, produces a flame, that lasts from ten minutes to half an hour. The men who perform this operation, are perfectly aware of the risk they encounter, and they are extremely careful how they execute it.

in some instances, the coffin may be turned round upon its axis, by the slightest touch of the finger, within a few hours after the lid has been soldered down, and holes are frequently bored through all the cases, over which the plate of the outer coffin is fastened; so that the gas may gradually escape into the room or vault in which it is deposited. When the coffin is not well secured, the lead will burst, and the gas become generally diffused. (¹)

An undertaker had placed a body in the vault of a church, at the north end of London; the odour emitted from the vault, and even from the church itself, shortly after, was so extremely offensive, that it was suspected the undertaker had not buried the body in lead; (²) upon examination, however, it was found that the stench proceeded from a pile of coffins placed in a corner of the vault, from which was exuding a very disgusting sanies.

(¹) EXTRAORDINARY INCIDENT AT NOURRIT'S FUNERAL.—The service at Marseilles, over the remains of Nourrit, was preceded by an incident that gave a shock to those who witnessed it. The leaden coffin, having been badly closed at Naples, burst, and exposed its contents in a state of far-advanced decomposition. A quantity of chlorate of lime was immediately sprinkled about, and a plumber engaged to make a new coffin. This was sufficiently solid to prevent a recurrence of the accident, but its weight was so great that it could not be raised upon the catafalque erected for it in the church, and was therefore left beneath, on the pavement.—(*Sun*, May 6, 1839.)

(*) From some remarks I have previously made, my readers will easily understand that many thousands of bodies have been deposited in places on the surface *without being placed in lead.* This is a monstrous abuse, and one that ought to have been an-

The following statement will prove, if proof, indeed, be wanting, the neglected condition of many of the vaults employed for burials, and the evils resulting from it :—

The vaults of a church, in the city, were in a

nihilated in its very origin. I have repeatedly entered places in which vast piles of coffins are deposited—the general smell of the atmosphere is extremely offensive ; here have I seen women of delicate organization, oppressed with grief for the loss of a beloved object, subject themselves to the action of a " malaria," given off in enormous quantities ;—possibly themselves specimens of walking sickness, led thither to contemplate the sad remains of what once was an affectionate husband—a beloved child, or relative. This should not be permitted,—*the power of resistance* ought not thus to be experimented with.

In objecting to the keeping of bodies when in lead, *unless placed in the earth*, and at a proper depth, I am aware that I differ with others upon this subject. Dr. Pascalis, previously quoted, says— " the structure of their coffins, in England, where, among the wealthy ranks, they generally use the churches for burial, seems well adapted to prevent the evils otherwise arising from their imprudent fashion of entombing corpses in the interior of churches : coffins of lead, soldered, lined, and cased in mahogany, or walnut, again in oak, and over all, covered with cloth or velvet, may be more secure against pestiferous vapours." Dr. Pascalis is here in error ; the coffin may be of lead, soldered, lined, and cased, yet the pestiferous vapours will frequently escape ; this security, therefore, is merely imaginary. Every person who has been accustomed to enter these places, can vouch for the truth of this assertion ; the disgusting stench in places largely ventilated, proves this. Very poisonous gases are the products of the decomposition of the dead ; they are generated under all circumstances, whether in the strong and expensive coffins of the rich, or in the frail and imperfectly made shells of the poor. These gaseous products of decomposition, condensed and compressed as they are, to considerably less

most revolting and dangerous condition, and had, for some years previously, occasioned considerable uneasiness to many of the parishioners; and in the more immediate vicinity of the church, the inhabitants complained of the nuisance—one of the churchwardens, thinking the cause of complaint might arise from external agencies, vitiating the atmosphere, ordered the windows, the roof, and every part of the building to be examined and made secure, and double doors to be made at the entrance of the church; notwithstanding these directions were obeyed, the stench became insupportable; many of the congregation were, at various times, compelled to leave the church, and some were seized with illness during service, and conveyed home.(¹)   The churchwarden, above alluded to, anticipating the source of the mischief, caused the vaults to be examined, when upwards of one hundred bodies were found in an active state of putre-

than half their volume, by continual increments from the decomposition of the general tissues, in some instances, may be retained by the mere strength of their cases; these, necessarily, must ultimately decay and burst, when the gases generated will be diffused throughout the vault in which they are deposited; whilst, in the grave yard, the borer of the grave digger, often employed in searching, is driven through the lid of the coffin, from which volumes of pernicious gases are continually emitted.

(¹) A highly respectable lady attended the church of ——— to hear a favourite evening lecturer,—the peculiar and disgusting stench from the vault beneath affected her so much that she was compelled to leave the church.

Many of my patients and friends have been annoyed in a similar manner.

faction. The workmen employed on this occasion, upon first entering the vault, were almost instantly prostrated upon the floor ; one poor fellow who had advanced further than the rest, was with difficulty saved ; he was dragged out by his companions, almost lifeless. The vault was ultimately cleared, and all the putrescent bodies were buried in a common pit, dug in the church yard.

A short time since, two bodies were deposited in a burying ground in my neighbourhood ; they were placed in one grave, the uppermost being only a few inches from the surface ; such was the intolerable stench arising from the bodies, that those engaged could not approach within several feet of the grave. I am convinced that many attendants at funerals, conducted under such circumstances, pay a fearful tax in the depreciation of their health—the almost inevitable result of their exposure to the exhalations of the dead. If these persons could be tracked to their homes, very frequently disease would be found, the result of exposure to a "malaria," whose dangerous effects, in this country at least, seem neither to be understood nor appreciated.

In a discourse preached by the venerable Hugh Latimer, Ex-Bishop of Worcester, in Lincolnshire, in the year 1552, the following passage occurs :—" The citizens of Naim had their burying places without the city, which, no doubt, is a laudable thing ; and I do marvel that London, being so great a city, hath not a burial place without : for no doubt it is an unwholesome thing to bury within the city, especially at such a time, when there be great sicknesses, and many die together. I think verily that many a man taketh his death in St. Paul's Church Yard (¹) and this I speak of experience; for I myself, when I have been there on some mornings to hear the sermons, have felt such an ill-savoured unwholesome savour, that I was the worse for it a great while after ; and I think no less—but it is the occasion of great sickness and disease."

Dr. Adam Clarke, in his Commentary on the raising from the dead the widow's son in the city of Naim, Luke vii. v. 12—15, has strikingly illustrated and confirmed the above remarks. The Jews always buried their dead *without* the city, except those of the family of David. No burying places should be tolerated *within* cities or towns, much less in or about *churches* and *chapels*. This custom is excessively injurious to the inhabitants; and especially to those who frequent public worship in such chapels and churches. God, decency and health, forbid this shocking abomination.

On the impropriety of burying in towns, churches, and chapels, take the following testimonies :—
" Extra urbem soliti sunt alii mortuos sepelire : Nos christiani, eos non in urbes solum, sed et in TEMPLA

(¹) At this period the congregation at St. Paul's Cross sat in the open air. There appears to have been a covered space at the side of the church, to which the preacher used to resort in inclement weather, called the *Shrowds or Shrouds.*

P

recepimus, quo fit ut multi fœtore nimis, ferè exanimentur."—SCHOETTGEN.—" Others were accustomed to bury their dead *without* the city : We Christians, not only bury them *within* our cities, but receive them even into our *churches!* Hence many nearly lose their lives through the noxious effluvia." —" Both the Jews and other people had their burying places without the city :—*Et certe ita postulat ratio publicæ sanitatis, quæ multùm lædi solet aura sepulchrorum :* and this the health of the public requires, which is greatly injured by the effluvia from graves."—*Rosenmüller.* From long observation J can attest, that churches and chapels situated in grave yards, and those especially, within whose walls the dead are interred, are perfectly unwholesome ; and many, by attending such places, are shortening their passage to the house appointed for the living. What increases the iniquity of this abominable and deadly work, is, that the burying grounds attached to many churches and chapels are made a source of *private gain.* The whole of this preposterous conduct is as *indecorous* and *unhealthy,* as it is *profane.* Every man should know, that the *gas* which is disengaged from putrid flesh, and particularly from a human body, is not only unfriendly to, but destructive of, animal life. Superstition first introduced a practice, which self-interest and covetousness continue to maintain.

Another circumstance intimately connected with the present mode of interment must be noticed. It is well known to grave diggers (¹) that in many cases it would be impossible to dig a grave in the midst of a mass of coffins, without taking great precautions. Some employ water, lime-water, &c. as absorbents; others throw down lighted paper, straw, shavings, &c. &c. thus the heavier gases are rarified by heat and driven off from the numerous laboratories of human putrefaction distributed in patches over the entire surface of London; and these gases once diffused in the atmosphere, are permanently mixed with it—are applied to the skin, and enter the lungs with every inspiration. It will be noticed also, from the description I have given of the humid condition of the soil in many grave yards, that no attention whatever has been paid to

(¹) I have conversed with many of these men in various parts of London; *there is not one* who has not at some time or other been more or less seriously afflicted in the execution of his work. Some have informed me that they have been obliged to fill up graves which they had attempted to dig—they were so overpowered by the effects of the gas. Many when employed in digging graves in cold weather, have noticed that the earth " reeks with noxious vapour"—condensed gases are at times perceptible to the eye; " they have a faintish smell"—irritate the nose and eyes—produce debility—and injure the appetite. At a depth of some feet from the surface, they are frequently insupportable; and every old and experienced grave digger keeps his head as erect as possible. If the man who fell in the grave in Aldgate had, with the usual selfishness of the craft, employed the ordinary precautions, two proofs less of the constantly poisonous nature of these gases would have been wanting. What are the evidences of their effects in a diluted state on the health of others exposed to their influence?

the kind of earth most suited to the purposes of inhumation. Now this should have been a primary object—putrefaction going on much more rapidly in moist than in dry situations.

I have adverted to the fact of bodies being placed within a few inches of the surface of the earth. I have shown that many thousands of bodies, or rather shells, piled one upon the other, are to be found in the vaults of churches and of chapels. It would appear, indeed, that mourners, after they have seen

> " The deep grave receive the important trust,
> And heard the impressive sentence—dust to dust,"

imagine that they have performed the last duty to their deceased friend : have they ever reflected that *they have deposited a centre of infection to the living ?*

It may be said that in many instances graves are dug to a great depth.([1]) I know that this is sometimes true, and I also know that an inducement is held out to the grave digger of an additional shilling or eighteen-pence for every additional foot of ground

([1]) In a very many instances deception is practised in respect to the depth of graves. To give an *appearance* of depth the earth is thrown up on each side to a considerable height, and planks are placed edgeways to prevent the earth from falling in.

A GRAVE DIGGER BURIED ALIVE.—A melancholy and fatal accident occurred at Kintore on Tuesday. The church officer, George Scott, was digging a grave, in which were to be interred the remains of a widow, whose husband had died six years ago. The new grave, which was close by the other one, had been dug about ten or twelve feet deep, and Scott was working in it when the large tombstone from the first grave

excavated beyond a given depth, but to accomplish this, it often happens that every opposing obstacle is cut through, and that the legs, the head, or even the half of a body are frequently dissevered.

Thus, among all classes of society, those who have been loved during life, and to whose remains the last affectionate duties have been paid, are, after they have passed, perhaps for ever, from our sight—though they may dwell in our remembrance —subjected to the most disgusting indignities. Even the enormous fees paid in some places cannot secure for our dead undisturbed repose. "The pride, pomp, and circumstance" of a funeral is a bitter jest—a biting sarcasm : the bodies of our wives, our daughters, our relatives, are to be exposed to the vulgar gaze, the coarse jests and brutal treatment of men, who being men, would not, dare not, execute the tasks imposed upon them.

Captain Marryat, in his "Diary in America," comments rather strongly upon the immorality of

slipped off, and, with a quantity of earth, fell upon Scott. In twenty minutes he was got out, but by that time was dead. The poor man bore an excellent character, and has left a family but badly provided for.—*Aberdeen Constitutional.*

DISGRACEFUL NUISANCE.—In the St. Mungo's New Burying Ground there is a pit or common grave for the remains of persons who die at the Royal Infirmary. This capacious receptacle is only covered by a few planks, and the stench emitted in hot weather is most insufferable. On Sabbath it was so abominable as to become matter of very general complaint on the part of persons passing to church within a hundred yards of the place.—*Glasgow Courier.*

the Americans, for suffering rail-roads to pass through *church yards*. He says, that "the sleepers of the railway are laid over the sleepers in death;" and asks, "would any engineer have ventured to propose such a line in England?" An engineer unquestionably would—he has proposed "such a line," and probably from the same motives as those ascribed to our neighbours across the Atlantic; but the decencies of life are not disregarded by a British public, and the attempt has failed. The Captain shall speak for himself. The *Manchester Times*, May 10, 1839, will give the commentary:—

" I was," says Captain Marryat, " I must confess, rather surprised, when in the railroad cars, to find that we were passing through a *church yard*, with tomb stones on both sides of us. In Rhode Island and Massachusetts, where the pilgrim-fathers first landed—the two States that take pride to themselves (and with justice) for superior morality-and a strict exercise of religious observances, they look down upon the other States of the Union, especially New York, and cry out, ' I thank thee, Lord, that I am not as that publican.' Yet here, in Rhode Island, are the sleepers of the railway laid over the sleepers in death ; here do they grind down the bones of their ancestors for the sake of gain, and consecrated earth is desecrated by the iron wheels, loaded with Mammon-seeking mortals. And this is the puritanical state of Rhode Island ! Would any engineer have ventured to propose such a line in England? I think not. After all, it is but human nature. I have run over the world a long while, and have always observed that people are very religious so long as religion does not interfere with their pockets ; but, with gold in one hand and godliness in the other, the tangible is always preferred to the immaterial. In America every thing is sacrificed to time ; for time is money. The New Yorkers would have dashed right through the church itself; but then, *they* are publicans, and don't *pretend* to be good."

In the line laid down for the Leeds and Manchester Railway, it was proposed to take in land belonging " to the Workhouse and to the Workhouse Burial Ground." The proposition was warmly disputed by the ley-payers, but the opposition to the measure in Parliament failed through the discrepancy of the evidence. However, at a meeting called by the Churchwardens, on the 9th May, 1839, the following resolution was passed :—

RESOLVED, " That as it now appears by the report of the Churchwardens and Overseers of the Poor that the Railway Company have announced in the Committee of the House of Commons sitting on the Bill that they intend to take a **very** small portion of the Burial Ground at the corner next to the Poor House land, at the corner next adjoining to the Burial Ground ; and that with regard to the Burial Ground they mean to traverse it on the surface, or nearly so, and that they will not disturb any of the bodies interred there ; and it also appearing that the Committee, acting on the impression that the resolutions of the meeting of the 26th of February were passed under the apprehension that bodies were to be disturbed, had decided that the opposition of the Churchwardens and Overseers was not sufficient to throw out the Bill on the preamble.

" That the objection to the interference with the Burial Ground, which is altogether unnecessary, is not removed by the course now pursued by the Railway Company ; that this meeting entirely disapproves of any invasion of that consecrated ground, and confirms the resolutions of the meeting of 26th February last."

In the course of the discussion at this meeting it was given in evidence that in twenty-five square yards on each side of the proposed line, 5,600 bodies were interred, and in fifteen yards on each side about 3,200." It was further proved, that "the grand total of interments in Walker's Croft from January 16, 1815 (the date of the consecration) to Friday the 22d February, 1839, is 32,245!

It would be very easy to enlarge the catalogue of these results. My object in detailing some of them is to direct the attention of the public to one particular source of disease, immediately or remotely affecting every individual of the empire. The public press has, from time to time, contributed its powerful aid, and endeavoured to awaken the strongest feeling of our nature, by pointing out the state of the grave yards in general, and exposing the loathsome abuses of some of the metropolitan burying grounds in particular.

The following Letter is taken from the *Weekly Dispatch*, of the 23d December, 1838 :—

THE CHURCH YARD NUISANCE.

MR. EDITOR,—Allow me to address you on a subject of very great importance to this metropolis—the burial of the dead. The recent shameful affair at St. Bartholomew the Great, Smithfield, which was so ably exposed in the *Dispatch*, I trust will plead my excuse; and I am further induced to do so, from a well-grounded conviction (after many years' experience as sexton of one of the most populous parishes in the kingdom), that nothing short of a Legislative enactment will prevent a desecration of the church yard. The cemeteries now established by various companies, do little or nothing towards the removal of the evil. This is not stated invidiously, it is the truth; for very few, if any, but the affluent, bury their dead in those receptacles, in consequence of the expense or want of conveyance thereto, the fees, &c.; nor are the bodies of the poor wanted there at all. The wealthy have ample accommodation in most parishes, and *as they bury mostly in leaden cof-*

fins, or deposit their deceased friends either in vaults, or in brick or deep graves, the mode employed by them is not obnoxious.(¹) Whereas the poor, who comprise two thirds of the mortality of the metropolis, continue to bury, and to be buried, in the crowded church yards and parish burying grounds, precisely as bad, and perhaps worse, than before these cemetery companies were established; for parishes, being deprived of their best burial fees, by reason of the said cemeteries, the vestrymen feel it incumbent on them to make the most of every inch of ground they possess, lest they should be compelled to make a rate on their parishioners to raise funds to purchase more ground; hence acts are winked at (until *publicly exposed*), and permitted to be done by their grave digger, at the bare contemplation of which humanity shudders. Several parishes in this metropolis bury twenty paupers per week, putting seven at a time in one grave, the last body being about three feet from the surface. Now this is the just cause of complaint. Of what use are the cemeteries? Do they, in any way, touch the evil? This is the great objection, and which requires immediate removal. I maintain they do not. I sincerely hope the Government, being the guardians of the public, will take this subject into their serious consideration. So important a one should not rest as it now does—a mere speculation, in the hands of private individuals, who look on it merely as a matter of pounds, shillings, and pence. It is suggested, that the Government should provide (in Paris the French Government do provide), four cemeteries, one in each quarter of the metropolis, and assign to every parish a portion thereof, in accordance to its population, the Government receiving the ground fee for every burial (except for paupers), in like manner as it is now received by the churchwardens, or parish authorities. The burial service should be performed in the parish church, of the parish in which the person died (or at his chapel, if a dissenter), the other lawful fees going to those who may be duly entitled thereto. Every parish should be compelled to provide a hearse, &c. to convey their paupers thereto, and a building, or covered shed should be erected to enable the mourners to dress and undress. It is conceived that the above plan, if carried into effect, would prove of immense benefit to the public, would lessen,

(¹) See the general remarks upon the abuses of interment, for a refutation of this highly dangerous error.

materially, burial expenses, and be a source of emolument and patronage to Government, as well as ornament to the nation.

A SEXTON.

[We have received more than fifty letters relating to the brutal mutilation of a corpse in the church yard of St. Bartholomew the Great, Smithfield; and we hope, with our correspondent, that some plan will be devised, to prevent a repetition of such an abominable outrage. The making, however, of church yards a source of patronage and emolument to the Government, is not a commendable feature in our correspondent's plan.]

It will be noticed that the general or particular remarks I have made in the course of these observations, in some instances prove, and in others originate suspicions, that dead bodies have in some places been deposited in such numbers that the spaces would have been utterly inadequate to receive them without the dispossession of previous occupants. The reflective portion of the community, upon a careful review of all the facts I have thought it necessary to detail, will be prepared to receive, and will cease to wonder, at an otherwise startling avowal—in one of the most influential of the literary and scientific periodicals of the present day, viz. that "Many tons of human bones every year are sent from London to the North, where they are crushed in mills constructed for the purpose, and used as manure."—*Quarterly Review*, No. XLII. p. 380.

It might reasonably be asked, by whom and by what authority have these supplies been furnished? From what grounds—public or private? Who have derived the emoluments? and to what purposes have the products been applied?

The extract given below from the life of a late eminent architect, Thomas Telford, Esq. will prove the insecurity of churches and other public buildings near to the walls of which interments are permitted, and the serious consequences that may result from the ignorant or parsimonious suggestions of parochial management :—

" While Mr. Telford resided in Shrewsbury Castle, under the patronage of Sir William Pulteney, an accident happened in the town, which ought to find a place in his biography. The collegiate and parochial church of St. Chad was founded by the kings of Mercia, in the seventh century, upon the final conquest of Shrewsbury by the Saxons, and the edifice was burnt in the reign of Richard the Second, by the carelessness of a plumber, who did not (as is too usual) escape with impunity. He was terrified at seeing the church in flames, and in his flight, attempting to ford the Severn, was drowned.

" The church was rebuilt, and after four centuries, in the year 1778, one of the four pillars which supported the tower in the middle of the church, was observed to crack in various places. These alarming appearances in the mother church of the town, created general anxiety, and Sir William Pulteney sent Mr. Telford to inspect the state of the fabric. His report to the assembled Parish Vestry was, that in consequence of graves having been dug in the loose soil, close to the shallow foundation of the N. W. pillar of the tower, it had sunk, so as to endanger the whole structure, and that the ruin of the church must speedily ensue, unless it were immediately secured by a thorough repair ; and he recommended that the bells should be removed, and the tower taken down forthwith, so as to permit the shattered pillar to be restored and secured, when relieved from the vast superincumbent weight. But the Parish Vestry, which met in the church on this occasion, exclaimed against such an expensive proposal, and some of them imputed interested motives to Sir William Pulteney's Scottish architect ; upon which Mr. Telford left them, saying,

' that if they wished to discuss anything besides the alarming state of the church, they had better adjourn to some other place, where there was no danger of its falling on their heads.'

" The Vestry then proceeded to direct a mason to cut away the injured part of the pillar, in order to underbuild it: and, on the second evening, after commencing this infatuated attempt, the sexton was alarmed at the fall of lime-dust and mortar, when he attempted to raise the great bell, for a knell on the decease of a parishioner. He left the church immediately, and the next morning (9th July, 1788), while the workmen were waiting at his door for the church key, the clock struck four; and the vibration produced by the motion of the chime-barrel, brought down the tower, which overwhelmed the nave of the church, demolishing all the pillars on the north side of it, and shattering the rest. It was now perceived that the walls and pillars of the church, as is seen in many such ancient structures, consisted of a mere outside coating of freestone, the interior being filled with a mass of rubbish, which crumbled into dust. Among this, and in the very heart of the pillars, were found stones, rudely carved, which were evidently of Saxon sculp_ture, and had been ruins of the ancient church, thus applied in building the second church in the reign of Richard II. The present church was entirely rebuilt in the interval, from 1788 to 1798, but in a manner which does no credit to the taste of the architect.

" The catalogue is lamentable of ancient churches which have fallen from want of attention, and especially from *grave digging*, near the walls and pillars. The middle tower of the abbey church of Selby fell in the year 1690, and destroyed half the church. So at Whitchurch, Salop, at Banbury, in Oxfordshire, Chelmsford, in Essex, and at Great Shelford, in Cambridgeshire. The city of Hereford was deprived of its principal ornament by the fall of the west tower and magnificent west portal of the cathedral, which suddenly became a heap of ruins, in the year 1781; and the workmanship was too expensive for modern imitation, although the west end of the cathedral has been decently restored by a good architect.

From the preceding statements, my readers will

be fully prepared to denounce the vicinity of burying grounds as prejudicial to the health and comforts of the living, and they will, no doubt, see the
propriety of the observations, and, where practi-
cable, act upon the recommendations so judiciously
given in a work published a few years ago in North
America, from which the following extract is taken :
—" Avoid as much as possible living near church
yards. The putrid emanations arising from church
yards are very dangerous; and parish churches, in
which many corpses are interred, become impregnated with an air so corrupted, especially in Spring,
when the ground begins to grow warm, that it is
prudent to avoid this evil, as it may be, and, in
some cases, has been, one of the chief sources of
putrid fevers, which are so prevalent at that season."

In concluding this division of my subject, I may
observe that, if from a deep conviction of the
necessity, I have entered upon a repulsive and disgusting detail, I have done so, because I have reflected that if the Legislators who regulate the criminal—the fiscal code of the country, can find no
ground for interference with the conduct of ignorant,
selfish, or unprincipled men—*that if private speculators have not yet been compelled to defer—to the
vast—the enormous—the utterly neglected* interests
of the PUBLIC HEALTH—another highly important
subject may yet find advocates amongst those who
reflect,—that the health and the morality of a people
are too inseparably connected to be dissevered.

RECAPITULATORY AND GENERAL REMARKS.

Having greatly exceeded the limits I had laid down at the commencement of this work, I must be brief in my concluding observations. It may be useful to pass over, in review, the principal features of the work.

It will be found that, with the exception of a few of the most barbarous tribes, all nations, through all ages, have venerated the burial places of the dead; that *inhumation* has been the prevailing custom, and that the vicinity of towns and cities has been most scrupulously avoided; it will be seen that, even among the Egyptians, where the custom of embalming was more generally adopted than in any other country, inhumation was practised among the common people; it is true that the custom of burning the dead succeeded to embalming, and that with the Greeks and Romans it was by no means uncommon: this custom, however, took its rise from a religious regard to the resting places of the dead. " It was observed that long wars, frequent transmigrations, the destruction and re-building of cities, might, with the revolution of time, overturn the whole surface of a country; *and that bones confided for several centuries, to the bosom of the earth, would then unavoidably be exposed upon the surface.* The FEAR OF SUCH A PROFANATION determined the practise of burning the dead; their repose, from that moment, was considered as secure."

Inhumation of the dead has, however, through all ages, been the prevailing custom; and a strict and affectionate regard to the sanctity of the tomb, is strongly characterised by costly monuments, or simple mounds, in every country of the civilized world. But the places selected for the burial of the dead were remote from cities, and far distant from the habitations of the living.

The *Jews*(¹) were very careful to remove the dead from their dwellings. They dreaded all communication with them, so much so that travellers were even forbidden to walk upon places where the dead were buried. Caverns and fields were destined for places of burial. The priests, it is true, were buried on their own estates, and sometimes in the tombs of kings; but every city always had its public cemetry outside the walls.

Inhumation was always more general in *Greece*

(¹) The burying places of this people, in and near London, are infinitely preferable to those of many other religionists; their mode of interment is, perhaps, not only least objectionable of any, but is decidedly the best.

than elsewhere, and the very salutary custom of conveying the dead to a distance from the cities, was inviolably preserved; indeed the whole religious doctrine and mythology of the Greeks tended powerfully to strengthen and support the laws which directed the bodies of the dead to be removed far from the habitations of the living.

The *Romans* entertained a religious veneration for the dead; and the places destined for sepulchre, were held particularly sacred. The law of the Twelve Tables clearly shows, that from the fourth century of the Republic, the custom of burning and inhumation were adopted as occasion might require, for it expressly forbids the burning or burial of any dead body in the city.

" Hominem mortuum in urbe ne sepelito neve urito."

Inhumation was established among the early *Christians,* and their dead were carried out of the city; but after Constantine had embraced the Christian religion, and peace had been established, innovations were admitted in the mode or place of interment. Constantine was allowed the privilege of being buried in the vestibule of a temple he had himself built; and the same honour was afterwards conferred upon many of his successors. It was subsequently granted to benefactors, who had provided liberally for the decorations of altars, and for the expenses incurred in performing the august ceremonies of religion, till at length, from veneration, ambition, or superstition, the abuse was carried so far, that interment, in the vicinity of churches, was granted to Pagans and Christians,—to the impious and the holy.

Attempts were unquestionably made by Emperors and Ecclesiastics, to correct this abuse. Theodosius the Great, in 381, published his celebrated code, in which he forbade the interment of the dead in the interior of cities, and even ordered *that the bodies, the urns, and the monuments which were in the city of Rome, should be carried without the walls.* The monks strictly observed the rules, and conducted themselves on this point, with the most austere severity; those who inhabited grottoes and deserts, were buried in forests, and in the heart of mountains. Walford, Abbot of Palazzolo, in Tuscany, was the first who, in the eighth century, wished to be buried in his own cloister. Sepulchres were soon afterwards introduced into churches, and further encroachments were rapidly made, till at length the prevailing custom was opposed to the established law, and the prerogative which was originally reserved for Emperors, became the portion of the lowest class of citizens, and that which was at first a distinction, became a right, common to every one.

It must be admitted, however, that in Catholic countries, the authorities of councils and the decrees of Popes, &c. have been directly opposed to interment in churches, and in the vicinity of cities and towns; but the desire of distinction penetrated into the interior of temples, and permission having become easy and general, distinction could only be acquired by the position of the tombs, and the magnificence of their decorations. A decree was issued by the Archbishop of Toulouse, in the reign of Louis XV. of France, against the admission of the dead within consecrated walls, and in places held sacred. He states, that in violation of the holy canons, interments in the metropolitan church had increased exceedingly, and that the air was sensibly contaminated by fetid exhalations from vaults. With a truly apostolic mildness, he reasons upon the dangers and the profanation of the practice, and as an excuse for his interference and to secure the docility and compliance of his diocese, says, " it was necessary that your eyes should be opened to your danger by repeated accidents, sudden deaths, and repeated epidemics. It was necessary that your own wishes, impelled by sad experience, should compel our interference; and that the excess of the evil should call, in a manner, for an excess of precautionary measures."

The whole of this ordinance, so far as it respects the subject of burial in churches or interment within cities, is well deserving a careful perusal, and attentive consideration. It will be found p. 63—76.

This ordinance, with those issued by the Bishops of other places, was laid before the French Court of Parliament for confirmation. The general complaint of the practice of burial in churches added weight to these ordinances, and the opinions of medical men, that the vapours exhaling from putrefaction, filled the air with chemical compounds, dangerous to health, and was productive of malignant diseases, confirmed by the epidemics which prevailed in the warm seasons, led to the appointment of scientific and professional men, to enquire into and report fully upon all matters connected with the subject; and an act of the Legislature was ultimately promulgated, commanding all towns and villages to discontinue the use of their old burial places, and to form others at a distance from the habitations of the living. This was followed up by a further decree, ordering high ground to be chosen for cemeteries, and every corpse to be interred at a depth of at least five or six feet.

The perseverance of the French Executive in carrying out their decrees is worthy of imitation.

In this country in particular, and more especially in the metropolis, the dangerous consequences of interment in densely populated neighbourhoods have, at different periods been experienced, and there is equal, and indeed much greater reason for the interference of the Legislature. The laws prohibiting interment within cities or towns throughout France, were founded upon the reasons urged by the Parliament of Paris, viz. that complaints were made of the infectious consequences of the parish cemeteries, *especially when the heats of summer had increased the exhalations,—that the air was then corrupted,—that the most necessary aliments would only keep a few hours in the neighbouring houses,—that this proceeded either from the soil being so completely saturated that it could not retain or absorb any longer the putrescent dissolution, or from the too circumscribed extent of the ground for the number of dead annually interred; and that the same spot was repeatedly used, and by the carelessness of those who interred the dead, often, perhaps, re-opened too soon.*

Presuming then, that the reasons here stated, were sufficiently cogent to influence the councils of a great and enlightened neighbouring country, to break through long established customs (interwoven with and confirmed by some of the strongest feelings of religion and humanity), and to prohibit, rigidly and impartially prohibit, the burial of the dead in the vicinity of dwellings destined for the habitations of the living,—I might reasonably hope that after the publication of the foregoing facts collected during a patient investigation, and some labour, the health of the metropolis would form a prominent feature in the measures of the Administration, and the attention of Parliament be early directed to enquire into and to adopt such measures as may avert threatening calamities and secure future sanatory improvements.

It must be remembered, that although my attention was originally directed to the condition of the burial places in my own immediate neighbourhood; and that although I have been prompted to extend my enquiries into the condition of those in other districts; yet—that taking into consideration the magnitude of the metropolis, the abuses here exposed (and many others that might be mentioned), however repulsive, disgusting, and immoral, would not amount to a tithe of the detail, were the investigation pursued under authority and judicious arrangement.

A well known Latin author has pithily remarked, on a particular occasion—

"Ex uno disce omnes."

It may, I fear, with truth be said, from the burial places of one vicinity—know all the rest. If so, let those who at present supinely look on and disregard the dangers threatening their poorer neighbours from these vast sources of disease, remember that pestiferous exhalations arising from the numerous infecting centres of the metropolis, are no respecters of persons; by the ever shifting gales of the moment, they may be visited, even in their chosen localities, their power of resistance experimented upon, and a severe penalty incurred— the punishment of their omission or neglect to avoid evils self-inflicted, and therefore removable.

" For the epidemics, whether influenza, typhus, or cholera, small-pox, scarlatina, or measles, which arise in the East end of the town, do not stay there; they travel to the West end, and prove fatal in wide streets and squares. The registers shew this; they trace diseases from unhealthy to healthy quarters, and follow them from the centres of cities to the surrounding villages and remote dwellings."—*Letter from Wm. Farr, Esq. to the Registrar-General.*

" The absence of plague from London has been ascribed by certain speculators to the enforcement of quarantine ; the cholera demonstrated the absurdity and inefficacy of the entire machinery of quarantine establishments, by crossing the cordons in every direction without any hesitation. It is time that this folly should be abandoned. Governments might shut out the four winds of heaven ; but pestilence will laugh at their precautions, while they retain the elements of pestilence in the bosom of their populations. Every fact with which science is acquainted tends to prove, that if we cannot exclude this subtle fire from our habitations, we can, to a certain extent, render them pestilence proof. A prosperous nation, whether scattered over a cultivated soil, or concentrated in well-constructed cities, has little to dread from the importation of cholera, plague, or yellow fever. In unhealthy places, the exclusion of one form of disease is of little advantage ; for other priests minister at the altars in its stead, and sacrifice the victims."—*Vital Statistics, by W. Farr, Esq.*

I am fully convinced, after the most mature reflection, that all the evils apprehended by the French Executive from the then prevailing custom of interment throughout France, may, in an increased ratio, be anticipated in this country—for, until very lately, the burial places of the metropolis and of the provinces have been under no superintendence. Public bodies or private individuals have been at liberty to allot grounds or to choose depositories for the reception of the dead, without limitation as to number, without controul as to locality, or the disposition of the charge with which they were intrusted; and it is proved that private individuals have availed themselves to an alarming and most injurious extent, of the ignorance or poverty of survivors.(¹) I have shown that in many places more bodies have been received than could possibly be interred without a brutal and indecent dispossession of previous occupants, and that the surrounding neigh-

(¹) It has, for a long period, been, and now is the custom, in a majority of the burying grounds belonging to the Establishment to impose double burial fees upon extra-parochial dead. This has resulted, in many instances, from the crowded state of the grounds, and it has been intended as a modest refusal. The question, it appears to me, has been, for a long period, between those who receive and those who offer the deposits; if *the depositaries* are satisfied, *the recipients*, perhaps, cannot be expected to remonstrate.

The " extra fees" have driven many, who were unable or unwilling to pay them, to seek other places; and there are many that the most fastidious pocket cannot complain of; walled grounds —enclosed receptacles, and low fees, have been a considerable inducement. I am acquainted with some places, one in particular. A private speculator built a chapel,—the ground rent was £50. per annum; he derived a better income from the dead than the living.

bourhoods must necessarily be endangered from the continuous emanations given off from vaults and grave yards, in which piles of bodies confined within their slender habitations are in some instances methodically, and in others, parsimoniously, arranged.

Here I may advert to the burial places in my own immediate vicinity. The " Green Ground" in Portugal Street, has been used for interment for a period "beyond the memory of man." Enormous numbers of dead have been deposited here, and yet the ground remains persistently level. It would be desirable to obtain an account of the number; no doubt, the particulars are on record, and could be furnished, of the burials within a given period. Should it appear that the ground has been overcharged, information should be given of the disposal of the earth—necessarily removed, to admit the continuous deposits. Bulk must occupy space. If removals of previous occupants should occasionally have been effected, it would be desirable to know, by what authority ?—at what period since the inhumations ?—and under whose immediate sanction these transfers have been made ? The general question might be asked, where have the remains of those removed been deposited—in what manner have the materials of which the coffins were made been used or appropriated? Unfortunately, it has long been notorious, that through the criminal neglect of survivors, the most disgusting violations of the dead have commonly passed off unnoticed and unpunished. On the surface of many grounds I have repeatedly seen coffin wood piled up for removal, and I could not refrain from wondering that this barefaced insult to the living, necessarily preceded by a disgusting exposure, and, too frequently, dismemberment of the dead, could have taken place with impunity, and that the perpetrators of these acts should escape unpunished. But these men, for necessity may have compelled them to the employment, are comparatively innocent. The abuse —the criminality of the act rests with those who superintend or connive at the transgression.

The above remarks are applicable to a vast majority of places I have examined, and of which I have not considered it necessary to detail the particulars. They indisputably prove, that the present system of inhumation, and it is not confined to the metropolis, is grossly immoral, and demands—imperiously demands, the interference of the Legislature to abolish or reform it. It might appear invidious to have selected the burial ground in Portugal Street, for particular remark; I have no intention to make this place the ruling theme of observation, because I am quite prepared to prove, that it is not an isolated instance; nor do I believe that it is a particular exception. It first occupied my attention in my professional enquiries, and I regret to find that it is but a specimen of the almost universal practice. The grounds in Russell Court and Drury Lane—the former belonging to St. Mary Le Strand, and the latter to Saint Martin's in the Fields, are excessively crowded with the remains of the dead—more especially that in Drury Lane—luxuriant in rank vegetation high as men's shoulders—its surface broken, uneven. and its general aspect repulsive.—It is a shabby, unchristian depository for the dead : an abomination to the living.

The burying ground in Russell Court measures 4,300 superficial feet, and that of Drury Lane about 11,000 superficial feet. It would not be difficult to state a limit to their capabilities. In the calculations made by eminent French authorities not more than 150 bodies should have been interred in the one, nor more than 500 in the other. Will the parish authorities confirm or contradict this calculation?

But what shall we propose upon the subject of

Private Burying Grounds? Unquestionably, that they be immediately and for ever closed; and that the proprietors, presuming that they have not acted illegally, receive a just compensation for their interest in the LAND ONLY; and that the dead there deposited remain undisturbed until a general cemetery or cemeteries be appointed to receive them, after a decent exhumation, and a solemn and appropriate transmission. It is true that a correct registry of burials may now be anticipated: why not a registry of the burial grounds (not one of which should be PRIVATE)—*the situation—the extent of ground—the numbers buried—and the period they have remained open?* A particular space can only receive a limited number; that number having been deposited, the ground should be closed, and no *disturbance* should on any account be permitted, but under the direction of an approved and responsible superintendent. I have been led to these remarks from considering the state of the private grounds which have fallen under my own observation, and as examples are always more influential than vague generalities, I would refer my readers to the particular description I have given at p. 154, of the management of the SPACE under the floor of Enon Chapel in Clement's Lane.

This space measures in length 59 feet 3 inches or thereabouts, and in width about 28 feet 8 inches, so that its superficial contents do not exceed 1,700 square feet. Now, allowing for an adult body only twelve feet, and for the young, upon an average, six feet, and supposing an equal number of each to be there deposited, the medium space occupied by each would be nine feet : if, then, every inch of ground were occupied, not more than 189 (say 200 in round numbers) would be placed upon the surface ; and admitting (an extravagant admission most certainly) that it were possible to place six tiers of coffins upon each other, the whole space could not contain more than 1,200 ; and yet it is stated with confidence, and by credible authority, that from 10,000 to 12,000 bodies have been deposited in this very space within the last sixteen years !

Those who by their ignorance, supineness, indifference, or neglect, have been instrumental to the disgraceful spoliations of the dead, which have been detailed in the preceding pages, might blush at the answer to the interrogatory,—what has become of this host of what once was intellectual?

Is this place a sample of other private burying places? it is, I fear, but an epitome of a numerous class. My enquiries have convinced me that private speculations should at all times be held in suspicion, and closely scrutinized.

A few years ago, an extreme sensation was very justly excited against abuses in the practice of *exhumation* for anatomical enquiries. What shall we say to the apathy of a people who have patiently and noiselessly admitted the wholesale exposure and dismemberment of their dead, and yet invoke the utmost penalties of the law upon the parties guilty of the exhumation of individuals? The avarice of man is too frequently ready to avail itself of circumstances, and when the living are insufficient to satisfy its insatiable appetite, scruples not to convert to its advantage the opportunities derivable from the disposal of the dead; pretexts have been substituted for arguments,—" burying places might be established, in which the dead would be securely and safely deposited, and in which survivors might be afforded the melancholy gratification, if doubtful of the presence of the body, of seeing the remains." Reasoning, we may presume in this manner, private individuals have set apart, in various localities in the metropolis, certain spots of ground for the purposes of interment,—and receptacles, called vaults, underneath places of worship, in which the coffins are deposited, and these latter depositories are, in some districts, preferred to the burying grounds adjoining them; this fact is strikingly illustrated in the description of a vault at the new Bunhill Fields burying ground, New Kent Road (p. 181), where upwards of 1,800 bodies are piled one upon another; the smell arising from this place, and from many others, notwithstanding its dilution with the atmospheric air, is at times intolerably offensive, and has more than once produced, in my own person, a feeling of nausea.

In a previous part of this work, I have stated, that *over some depositories for the dead, children of both sexes are educated.* In some instances, indeed, School Rooms have been erected or employed immediately over the emanations given off by human putrescency; and in others the spot chosen for the purposes of education is in the immediate vicinity of such emanations.

This hazardous exposure of the susceptibilities of youth to malarious influence must be the result of ignorance or thoughtlessness on the part of those who have projected so unwise and dangerous a measure. It cannot, for one moment, be imagined that the benevolent feeling which prompted the desire to promote the moral improvement of the young, would, intentionally, be instrumental in exposing them to influences that must inevitably deteriorate or destroy the general health and bodily vigour. I venture to anticipate that the mere allusion to the circumstance will be sufficient either to occasion the removal of these places of instruction, or that the causes, operating to render them so highly objectionable and destructive, will be annihilated. Children, the miniatures of an enlarged existence, are a valuable property of the Empire;—remotely they may contribute to its power or resources—to its strength or its weakness.

" The number of children reared has doubled within the last century, and the mortality between 20 and 30, appears on the increase; so that, unless the hygienic precautions, very ably enforced by Dr. Clark, be followed, it is not improbable that an increase of weakly bodies and of consumption may be observed."—(Vit. Stat.)

" If half the children formerly cut off at an early age, in England, be now reared, and form part of the adult population, while the annual deaths between 20 and 30, instead of being 7.6, or 9.1, or 8.9 per 1,000, as in Carlisle, Belgium, and Sweden, are 10.1; it will appear that a vast number of weakly children are every year introduced into the English population, and that, unless proper means are taken to fortify the constitution in manhood, the relative vigour will not increase in the same ratio as the population."—(Idem.)

I have stated at p. 150, that in Clement's Lane, and at the upper end, which adjoins Clare Market, and is called Gilbert Street, the disease called typhus fever "had made the most destructive ravages." The mortality in this lane has been, at periods, excessively great; the instances of sudden death have been numerous, and cases of modified disease,—examples of action without power,—involving, perhaps, no particular organ or tissue, have very frequently come under my notice. The inhabitants occupying the houses looking over the open space of the burying ground in Portugal Street, have, perhaps, latterly suffered most. The exhalations of the grave yards in this neighbourhood, it may reasonably be inferred, have increased the malignancy and putridity of disease; the poor man's residence overlooks his grave. May it not, then, fairly be stated, that cause and effect have here been constantly in operation, and constantly increasing in the ratio of the mortality. Can we believe that the power of infection ceases when the animating principle has departed,—when the solids are contaminated,—when the blood,

R

poisoned at its source, and in its whole current affected, ceases to stimulate the central organ of the circulation—the heart? If, during the period in which life and death are struggling for the mastery,

> " Whilst the slow staggering race which death is winning,
> Steals vein by vein, and pulse by pulse away,"

the living can be infected by contact or proximity, —shall they not be diseased by the bodies from which the conservative principle has departed? When the poison that has destroyed life, is disengaged by the decomposition of the tissues with which it was in combination,—when, as in severe forms of typhus fever, the vitality possessed by both solids and fluids, is of the lowest degree, we may fairly conclude, that in proportion to the degree of putrescency evidenced during life, will be the degree of danger to the living, from the emanations of the dead.

" Death, in its most common form, is the effect of disease in the brain and spinal marrow, the blood, the lungs, the heart and blood-vessels, the bowels. Fever, inflammation, and various morbid products infect the whole system, and prove fatal, sometimes, by the mechanical injury they do, but more frequently by an alteration of the chemical, physical, and vital processes. Persons die of inflammation in the stomach before its structure is disorganised: fever is at times fatal without producing any essential lesion of the vital part. Cholera, plague, and other epidemics, extinguish existence as rapidly as poison."—(Vital Statistics.)

Doctor Armstrong is of opinion that typhus fever is synonymous with the term "plague" of the older writers; the latter term was employed to designate almost any severe epidemic disease indiscriminately. Now it is confined to a form of disease, or fever, in which buboes, carbuncles, and petechiæ appear, or in other words, enlarged axillary, inguinal, and other glands, or obstinate boils; the same appearances are present in some cases of typhus. The following extract is taken from his work on the practice of physic:—

" My former belief was, that typhus fever arose from human contagion. But I have lived to feel it a duty incumbent upon me entirely to alter that opinion. The following case affected me deeply, and first led me to review my opinion on the subject, —the opinion I mean, which I then entertained with regard to the origin of typhus fever:—About six years ago, and shortly after I had published the third edition of my work on typhus fever, in which I had strenuously maintained the doctrine of human contagion, I met a case of intermittent fever. In a few days more it put on the continued character, and the patient died, with all the most malignant symptoms of typhus fever.

"This case made a powerful impression on my mind, and I could not help asking myself whether it was not possible that the common ague of this country, the marsh remittent fever, and continued typhus fever, might be one and the same affection, modified by certain circumstances? I determined, at any rate, to re-investigate the subject; for I suspected I might have taken up, as a prejudice, at College, the doctrine of contagion, and might have acted on that prejudice as a sacred truth. Few men have more contemptuous views of black-letter learning and the dogmata of schools; yet the opinion clung to me closely, and I parted with it gradually, if not with regret. I investigated the subject afresh, resolved, if possible, to arrive at the plain truth, whatever it might be; and in six years the result has been, that *I am perfectly convinced that what is commonly called typhus fever does arise from malaria*, or marsh effluvia; that it is intermittent, remittent, and continued; that it arises from infection ; and that it does not originate from human contagion. It should be remembered that infection is not contagion. It is a state of atmosphere, produced by the surface of the earth and the air, which is limited to a certain space; and persons breathing it are subject to certain modifications of a similar disease."

In another place the Dr. observes, " an old nurse, in the Fever Hospital, told me that in cases of typhus fever she had frequently observed bubo, but that it had always been in severe cases. Since then I have met with many cases of typhus fever in London, *where there has not only been a distinct bubo in the groin, but there have also been carbuncles in different parts of the body.* I have seen many such cases in the Fever Hospital, and many in private practice."

" A German physician, who was sent to England by the Emperor of Austria, and who had been in various parts of the world, told me that in Turkey he observed the pestis put on an intermittent, a remittent, and a continued character, and that his firm opinion was, that it arose from malaria."

" A friend of mine, from the pest-house, at Constantinople, came to the Fever Hospital; I took him to the bedside of a patient, labouring under typhus fever, and said, what do you call *this case? He replied, plague.*"

" And it cannot be thought strange, that most who took the contagion, should have a fever, to those who consider the nature of a nitrous spirit, especially when degenerated, and that from the most slight cause it will take fire and excite heat ; and the fever accompanying this present sickness was of the worst kind, both on account of its state and periods, sometimes imitating a quotidian, and at others a tertian."—*(Hodges on the Plague.)*

I shall close these quotations with the observations of Dr. Brown, under the article Plague, in Encycl. of Pract. Med., in reference to the case occurring on the *Banks of the Tigris*, given in p. 11 of this work.

" The strongest analogy with plague which we have any where found, occurs in the following example of disease, induced, as it would appear, by exposure to the effluvia of common putrifying animal matter."

Thus, the opening a grave in which a body had been interred two or three months previously, produced, in two instances, symptoms of a disease having the ' strongest analogy with plague,'—so strong is the analogy, that the identity cannot be denied. The poison that destroyed two lives, in Aldgate, gave a longer respite on the banks of the Tigris; the men who dug the grave for their deceased shipmate, were unfortunate in the selection of its locality. Can those who, in too many places dig graves in London, who, provided with iron borers to " search," as it is called, for space for new customers, offer the excuse of ignorance? they know perfectly well that " *necessity is the mother of invention.*" They know that the searcher has a double purpose to execute; it is not employed in every instance, as an exploring instrument, but in being driven through the lid of the coffin, it gives exit to the compressed and highly destructive gas. Now if these gases produced, in the cases we have under review, the results we have recorded, they can produce effects, varying in degree, on the health of those who are exposed to their influence.

I have, I think, sufficiently explained to my readers the management of certain localities; it is a rule with grave diggers to avoid as much as posible inhaling the gases given off by the putrefaction of the dead. When bodies are inhumed, and the slower dissipation of the products is interfered with by the pick axe or the shovel, *the grave is left open until the surrounding atmosphere has diluted the poison,* or at least the lighter products are driven off; the heavier gases, those that destroyed the men in Aldgate,—are driven off by heat,—or absorbents are employed. In some instances they are " laded up in buckets," and poured out on the surface, but in the majority of instances, heat is employed.

I have stated at p. 156, that meat, exposed in a house in the neighbourhood of Enon chapel, after a few hours became putrid; (¹) independently of this fact, there is something extremely disgusting and repulsive in the thought that food for the living should be exposed to the influence of so polluted an atmosphere.

The evidence afforded by medical men, in reply to the queries of the Poor Law Commissioners, will tend to elucidate my subject. Sources of disease, constantly in operation, and of fearful magnitude, have been unequivocally pointed out. Mr. Bullen, p. 141, expressed his opinion, that the burial places in his district (and some of them are in a most disgusting condition), are the chief sources of pestilental disease.

(¹) See the preamble to the Act for abolishing interments in the vicinity of towns and cities throughout the French dominions, p. 77, viz. " that the most necessary aliments will only keep a few hours in the neighbouring houses," &c.

Mr. Evans, p. 143, says " the Poor Law Commissioners have been rightly informed that a very *malignant typhus fever* has prevailed here for some time past, and, indeed, rages now as bad as ever, and I think, more fatal in its course. In looking over my books, I find that, in the space of nine months, I have attended upwards of five hundred pauper cases; but *I cannot trace the disease to any local cause, for we have in the parish of St. George very good drainage through the parish, and very little accumulated filth, with the exception of Falcon Court, White Street, Noel's Court, Hunter Street, and Peter Street, Mint, but here the disease does not exist more severe than over the parish in general.*"

Had this gentleman inspected the burial places in his district (enormously overcharged as they are with dead), he would, I am convinced, have discovered vast sources of disease, in comparison with which the sewerage of the district (if even imperfect), could bear no proportion.([1])

([1]) Dr. Mead, in " a short discourse concerning pestilential contagion, and the methods to be used to prevent it, London, 1720," makes the following observations : " It has been remarked in all times that putrid exhalations from the earth, and, above all, the corruption of dead carcases lying unburied, have occasioned infectious diseases.

" The advice to keep at a distance from the sick is also to be

Dr. Armstrong states, that " Mons. Gaspard has shown, by experiment, that putrid animal or vegetable matter introduced into the blood, occasions a fever of the typhoid, or typhus form; and " so convinced am I," adds Doctor A. " of the truth of the doctrine of malaria, and a local taint, or contamination of air, that I believe, that with the aid of the Legislature, I could go far to annihilate typhus fever in the British metropolis."

The ravages made by fever of various kinds, in the districts of Bethnal Green and Whitechapel, have been truly alarming. The following particuculars are taken from the Fourth Report of the Poor Law Commissioners :—

" But the magnitude of the result in London, if that magnitude be estimated by the numbers attacked, is not slight. From returns received from the Bethnal Green and Whitechapel Unions, it ap-

understood of the dead bodies, which should be buried at as great a distance from dwelling houses as may be, put deep in the earth, and covered with the greatest care."

" They should likewise be carried out in the night, while they are yet fresh and free from putrefaction, because a carcass not yet beginning to corrupt, if kept from the heat of the day, hardly emits any kind of steam or vapour."

pears, that during the last year there occurred of fever cases,

In the Bethnal Green Union......2,084

In the Whitechapel Union........2,557

Total...4,641

" Thus, it appears, that the medical officers attached to these two Unions alone have attended no less than 4,641 fever cases. But these returns include only the persons attacked with fever, who applied to the parish for relief. *Fever, it is notorious, has prevailed extensively in both these districts among people above the rank of paupers, among people of the middle class, and, in numerous instances, even in the families of the wealthy.*"

"In one union, two of the relieving officers have, within a short time, been carried off by fever, caught in a similar manner. (¹) The extent of the pressure

(¹) The following apposite, and eloquent observations are taken from the *Lancet* of 28th July, 1838 :—

The Poor Law Commissioners say—" Several Officers have fallen victims to the prevalent disease. The excuse from one Union, for answers being only given by one medical officer is, that the other had fallen a victim to typhus, caught in the course of the performance of his duties in the infected neighbourhoods.

" Mr. Garrett, surgeon, of St. George's, East, and Mr. Doubleday, of High Street, Borough, were labouring under typhus when the Report was made ; Mr. Gozna, of Saint

upon the rates, in many instances, arising from the causes specified, may be judged of from the following return from the parish of Bethnal Green, which has a population of 62,018 :—

" Number of fever cases attended by the medical officers of this parish, ' St. Matthew, Bethnal Green,' *for one quarter*, ending March 25, 1838.

" Total,...521.

" The cost of in-door cases is at least 5s. weekly, averaging 20s. for each case, before the patient is sufficiently recovered. Twenty-six cases were ad-

Martin-in-the-Fields, died from that disease ; Dr. Fergus, the talented officer of St. George's Parish Infirmary, died from fever ; and Dr. Simms was last week cut off by the same unmitigating malady. But our space would fail if we attempted to enumerate the names of one-tenth of the victims—the young, the full of promise, the rife in strength—who have fallen in the discharge of their duties. Others have rushed to their post ; but the cries of the forsaken widows and orphans are lost in the tumult and murmur of the world. The soldier who destroys his fellow-creatures, is recompensed, pensioned, and covered with glory, but the physician of the poor has no reward during his life—has no monument when he ceases to exist ; he is suffered to die unregarded and unapplauded,—looking death full in the face,—struggling with a deadlier enemy to his country than the foe—whom the soldier encounters under the sun, with floating banners, and music, and all the ' pomp and circumstance of war.' Is this equitable and wise ? Does a generous nation owe to the memory of these men nothing ? Should they be allowed to foresee in hopeless delirium—that their children will remain unnoticed, unpitied, unsuccoured by the persons in whose service they have fallen ?"

mitted into the London Fever Hospital, at the cost of £27. 6s. to the parish for the last quarter, in addition to the number above reported."

" By the returns from the Bethnal Green and Whitechapel Unions, it appears that the extra expense for fever cases *for the quarter* ending Lady-day, 1838, is,

	£.	s.	d.
"To the Bethnal Green Union ...	216	19	0
"To the Whitechapel Union	400	0	0
	616	19	0

" Thus, at the rate of last quarter, there will be incurred, during the present year, for the relief of fever cases, *in these two parishes alone*, the sum of £2,467. 16s.

" *So extreme has been the social disorder, and so abject is the poverty of some of the places which are now the seats of disease, that great numbers of the dwellings have been entirely abandoned by the leaseholders.*"

This statement affords a painful proof of the close, the inseparable connection existing between physical agencies producing disease, and their demoralizing results. Though the power of mere circumstances can never be absolute over a rational and responsible being,—though we never can be quite bereft of the means of making ourselves better or worse ; still it is not to be denied, that upon circumstances depends the moral and social elevation or depression of all sorts and conditions of mankind in the mass. Let circumstances be favourable, virtue and happiness will prevail,—let them be adverse,—vice and misery will abound.

It is computed that half the deaths of the inhabitants of the globe are produced by fever of various kinds—the amount—or intensity of this in a district will pretty accurately indicate the condition of the air respired by its inhabitants. I am aware that in localities where masses of human beings are impacted—where no attention is paid to ventilation—where decaying refuse or excrementitious matter is allowed to accumulate (and that this is too frequently the case, I shall take an early opportunity of proving), the inevitable result must be the deterioration of the surrounding atmosphere : this deterioration having attained a certain degree of intensity, leaves the evidences—the records of its results in the pages of the historian—in the huge masses of misery it has created—and in the wide spreading desolation it has occasioned.

It is a hackneyed argument—that London is comparatively healthy. Those who thus argue will not, I think, attempt to prove, after the exposition given in these pages, that the aggregate health of its inhabitants is at its maximum, and that is incapable of further improvement by well-considered sanatory regulations.

These observations are corroborated by the following statement taken from the *Lancet* before quoted :—

"In the census of 1831 it was found that 4,019,161, or 29 per cent. of the entire population of England and Wales, resided in cities having more than 10,000 inhabitants. The population of the same class of cities in 1801, amounted to 2,381,129—or nearly 27 per cent. of the population. This simple numerical statement demonstrates the importance of devoting the strictest attention to the salubrity of our cities, where such masses of families are accumulated ; and the fact that the mortality is 40 per cent. higher in cities than in the entire population, ought no longer to be overlooked, as the causes of death are well known, and the remedy is easy of application. If the annual mortality were reduced from 2.84 per cent. in cities, to 2.03—the average rate of dying applicable to the entire population—the deaths every year in cities would amount to 82,174, instead of 114,963 ; and who knows but that among the 32,789 annually saved, a father, a mother, a child, a friend, may not be found ? Every member of the community is directly concerned in this question.

"The excessive mortality of city populations has sometimes been ascribed exclusively to vice and starvation, but this is in direct contradiction with a remarkable series of observations on the mortality of 2,034 labourers in the East India Company's service during the ten years ending with 1834. The mortality under 40 was not so high as in the general population of London, because the greater part of the labourers were healthy men, selected, and admitted into the service between the ages of 20 and 35 ; after 50 it was higher than the general mortality of London. These men were well supplied with food and clothing; their work, without being hard, ensured regular muscular exercise ; in sickness they had rest and proper medical attendance ; yet between the ages of 40 and 50 the mortality was 67 per cent., and between 50 and 60 as much as 82 per cent. higher than the mortality at the same ages in all England. Such facts as these annihilate the supposition that the increased mortality in cities is due to want of food and greater misery ; nor, can it be admitted, although these men drank freely, that their moral habits differed so greatly from those of country labourers as to account for their greater mortality.(¹) The source of the excessive sickness and mortality must be sought in the generation of effluvial poisons."

I have now, however imperfectly detailed the particulars of a long and laborious investigation. I have placed before my readers a general history of the modes of interment in different nations, from the earliest periods. I have shown at what times, and on what occasions, encroachments in the original modes of burial have taken place ; I have pointed out many of the destructive consequences that have resulted, and I have given, with much minutiæ, a statement of the gross abuses and immoral tendencies arising from the practices now prevalent in the burial places of the metropolis.

With the full conviction that I have, to the best of my ability, performed an important public duty,

(¹) See Macculloch's " Statistics of the British Empire," art. Vital Statistics.

in submitting the result of my labours to the judgment of my countrymen, I look forward with confident anticipation to the cordial co-operation of my fellow citizens, and also to the assistance of the Legislature to crush, or effectually reform the present system of burial,—a system fraught as much with insult to the dead, as with extreme danger and affliction to the living.

The weighty import of the matters contained in this work, induced me to hope that the subject would have been taken up by the Executive; and, therefore, in April last, I addressed a letter to the Right Honble. Lord John Russell, the then Secretary of State for the Home department, and requested the opportunity of personally communicating with his Lordship. I received an answer stating, that his Lordship was so much occupied with public affairs, that he could not comply with my request, but that his " best consideration should be given to such remarks as appeared to me important on the subject of the diseases which prevail in the metropolis." In accordance with his Lordship's wishes, I transmitted a copious general statement of the particulars now published, but I have had no intimation that the statement was received.

I am happy to see, that since the announcement of this work, the attention of the Press has been attracted to this subject; with so influential an advocacy, a sanatory change in the system of burial must be effected; the flagrant abuses, now unblushingly, and with impunity, practised, must be annihilated.

FINIS.

J. HICKLIN, PRINTER, PELHAM STREET, NOTTINGHAM.

Printed in the United States
71060LV00001B/81

9 780766 162495